Courageous Parents

Opposing Bad Influences, Impulses, and Trends

Haim Omer

For information, contact

MSI Press, LLC
1760 Airline Hwy, #203
Hollister, CA 95023

Library of Congress Control Number: 2019918065

ISBN: 978-1-950328-01-7

Table of Contents

Introduction

This book is both a summary of my 25 years of work in the field of parenting and an attempt to contend with the massive challenge facing parents today. It is a challenge with no equal in all of human history. That is because parents today are weakened by a number of factors while children face a slew of unprecedented temptations and risks.

Never before have children faced the deluge of temptations they do today. Children are flooded with a stream of seductions and stimulations resulting from affluent society, harmful trends, and addictive substances, which are ever-present. The temptations are all the more alluring because of their dissemination through advertising means that reach children at all hours of the day and night, not only through television but also through the smartphones to which children's eyes and ears are glued at every moment.

Just when our children are so dangerously flooded by alluring messages, there has been a drastic drop in parental status, due to far-reaching changes in social structure and educational values. Parents are weaker primarily because they are lonelier. The shrinking of the extended family is a worldwide phenomenon. Parents are much less supported by grandparents, siblings, and neighbors. The rate of divorce and single-parent families have risen sharply. Today's small family is increasingly isolated in its own apartment. A well-known proverb says "it takes a whole village to raise a child." That village has completely disappeared from the landscape. The community has stopped playing a constructive role in the lives of children and families.

Parents are also weaker because much of the authority they once wielded has been taken away from them both by society and by today's values and educational ideals. It is a positive process in its own right—after all, corporal punishment and achieving obedience through force, once accepted, are negative phenomena whose eradication we are justifiably proud of. However, it is doubtful parents have received means to fill the vacuum left in their wake. To the contrary, there is a feeling that not only are other measures to rear children absent, but when parents turn to the ways of the past, they are astonished to discover everybody is up in arms against them, even further eroding their authority.

Added to this is a sweeping cause of weakness: the Internet. In the past, adults represented knowledge and wisdom. Today that role has been assumed by the Internet. Children are more connected to the Internet and current in their knowledge of social media than their parents. Today the source of "wisdom" is literally in children's hands. Sometimes, parents are tempted to yank their children's devices out of their hands, as a punishment among other reasons. They say "it's the only punishment that works." The problem is that it does not work and parents are unable to sustain it.

The aggregate of my work culminates in one single image: the role of the parental anchor. Against the rising drift of children in dangerous directions and away from parents, parents must find a way to anchor themselves to their "parental ground," to serve as anchors for their children. The parental anchor provides not only security but also a strong and positive attachment to and for the child. It is the guarantee that the child will have a present and stable parent and not be abandoned helplessly to the maelstrom. Drift and anchor are the leading metaphors of this book. Each and every paragraph describes an aspect of the interplay between the two. My ultimate goal is to help parents reclaim the role of anchor for their children.

Reclaiming the role of anchor is an act of courage. But one cannot be courageous when completely steeped in weakness and confusion. This book is not only an injunction to parents to become courageous but also a detailed guide on where they can find the sources of this courage. In my work with thousands of families, I have witnessed how parents who had lost their stamina, their belief in themselves, and sometimes even their will found their way back to their own parenthood. Had these parents been told at the start that they would have found the courage to do what they did, they would have smiled in disbelief.

Hod Hasharon, Israel
July 2019

Chapter One

The Challenge of Parenting Today

Today, being a parent is very hard. Why? The parental role has lost its clarity. Simultaneously, parents have lost their support systems, and children are now exposed to more temptations.

What is the role of a parent?

In the past the job consisted of sustaining children and teaching them values and basic life and work skills. Clearly, a parent who fulfilled those jobs was a good and responsible parent. In short, parents instructed; children respected and obeyed. Countless rules, customs and laws established the elevated status of parents and validated this relationship. Everyone accepted the assumptions behind these expectations. Parents, teachers, religion, the law, and the broadcast and written media, all fully supported them.

Today things are far from being so clear. Validation of these former assumptions has eroded, making the parental role fuzzier. The parental role is both less clear for the parents and less validated by their environment.

The loss of clarity has rendered parents confused and hesitant. Today's parents suffer much more from doubts, dilemmas and guilt. The question "where did we go wrong?" is more common than ever. "Confused parents" are no less loving, devoted or caring parents. It might be to the contrary: in our complex world, parents who do not experience some confusion and doubt might not be alert to the difficulties of the modern world and the dangers that their children face. Still, parental confusion can weaken parents significantly, especially when parents face challenges that demand they take a firm and decisive stance. In such situations confused parents will struggle to find a firm and stable basis for their parenting. This increases the chances that the child will go astray.

What caused loss of clarity in understanding parent's role?

Parents find themselves in states of confusion, doubt and helplessness not only because childrearing values have become less clear and consensual but also because today they face new and bigger challenges than ever before. These challenges have to do with family structure, social composition and technological developments.

Changes in Family Structure

The main changes in family structure have to do with

- the rise in the divorce rate;
- the percentage of single-parent families;
- and the decline in support by the extended family.

Rise in Divorce Rate

Divorce has changed from a marginal phenomenon to commonplace throughout the developed world. Divorced parents often have less support and more dfficulty coordinating their roles with one another.

Rise in Single-Parent Families

A parallel phenomenon is the rise in the number of single and sometimes very young mothers and fathers. Countless studies show that in such families the risk of behavioral problems rises while the parents' ability to deal with them declines. Two parents living together can stand more firmly against the pull of destructive forces than a single or divorced parent.

Decline in Support of the Extended Family

Changes in the extended family also undermine parental stability. In the past, the nuclear family received more support from grandparents, uncles and older children. Childrearing today has increasingly become the sole responsibility of the parents, or even of a single parent. Children grow up less frequently inside an extended family and more often in a one-on-one relationship. This may also undermine parental stability. It has been proven, for instance, that in families where grandparents are involved in childrearing in addition to the parents, the risk of delinquency is lower. The presence of the grandparents, added to the attention of the parents, provides a sense of support and vigilant care.

Growth of Cities

The growth of cities makes raising children safely difficult for parents. Large cities project anonymity, offer a profusion of temptations, and create convenient opportunities to "get lost." Today's children are not only flooded with much more enticing and varied temptations than before, but also they can more easily evade the parental radar and blend into the woodwork. In the past, if the child was not in the parents' immediate field of vision, the chances that someone they knew would see them was much greater than today. Children felt seen and knew that their problematic behaviors could not remain hidden for long. In the big city, things are completely different: under the cover of anonymity of the modern metropolis, misbehavior can remain hidden from view.

The impact of the big city is felt in the suburbs as well, with boys and girls making an excursion to the city one of their preferred pastimes. The reason is not only that the city offers more possibilities but also offers more cover. Thus, the city becomes a giant magnet that pulls youth into it.

Technological Development

Another challenge to the parents' standing is rapid technological development, which places parents in a position of weakness vis-à-vis their children. The most obvious technological changes include, of course, the computer, the Internet, and the smartphone. Whereas in the past parents could assume that their general knowledge guaranteed them an advantage over their children, in the digital world, parents increasingly find themselves at a disadvantage, in terms of both knowledge and influence. The influence of cell phones makes parents feel increasingly marginalized:

- As the cell phone grabs their children's ears and eyes.
- Parents' messages pale because the cell phone broadcasts much shinier messages.

- Parenting time is shortened because the cell phone takes up growing portions of their children's time and attention.

Among all the erosion factors that threaten parental standing, the cell phone dominates. Its influence is felt all the time because even when children are not physically looking at it, they ask themselves what is new on the social networks and wait impatiently for the moment they can catch up. Time outside of the cell phone turns into wasted time in their minds. In this situation, the parents might turn into representatives of the irrelevant, uninteresting, non-current world, dinosaurs headed for extinction in the child's mind.

Patterns of "Helplessness"

With the proliferation of temptations, sources of influence and opportunities of evasion, parents' ability to stabilize and direct their children is gradually impaired. The child is carried away by the tidal wave of the modern era, and the parents remain helpless. For parents to recover from their state of weakness, they must be able to identify how they are being weakened. The following sections describe some of the main forms of parental weakness with several questions all parents can ask themselves:

- Repetitive attempts to explain and persuade without achieving the desired outcome;
- resorting to emotional responses;
- giving up own space, time, and goals; and
- marginalization.

Do I repeatedly explain and persuade, explain and persuade, but to no avail?

The following are comments from parents who are caught up in this pattern:

Greta: It is always important for me to explain to my children why I do what I do and why a certain behavior is wrong. I'm sure if the child understands, it will get better. It worked great with my two older children. Even if it was sometimes hard for them to understand, in the end they did, and things got better. But with my younger daughter, it doesn't work. Even when she was in grade school, I had the feeling she wasn't listening, wasn't absorbing, or didn't want to understand though somehow in the end it would sink in. Since she has reached puberty, things have changed. She blocks her ears, shouts at me to "shut up!" or just lets me understand that everything I say goes in one ear and out the other. How can I explain to her that she is actually hurting herself?"

Sam: No matter what I say to him, he makes counter-arguments. He's really good at it, a little lawyer. Since he was little, he questioned whatever we said, asking "why?" Even the smallest thing would lead to a long discussion. Honestly, it's very hard to withstand his arguments. He presents us with reasons, justifications and examples to which we have no response.

Explanation and persuasion are central processes in education because parents are the principal mediators of the world for the child. This role provides authority for the parent—positive or negative.

Parents who display positive authority explain their positions. Thereby, they increase the chances their positions will be accepted and adopted.

In contrast, the authoritarian parent not only offers no explanation but also turns lack of explanation into a trademark of their authority. Their only explanation is: "Do it because I said so!" The assumption is that obedience must be blind or else it is not real obedience. This form of authority has lost its legitimacy and has no place in childrearing.

That said, explanations can become futile, and endless discussion can become a mechanism that prevents decision and action. Many children understand this well and know how to draw out discussions endlessly because they know that as long as their parents are talking they are not acting. The more parents explain and preach, the more they dilute their standing and presence through their continual talking.

Parents can determine to what extent they fall into the chatter trap by learning to listen to themselves.

- Do they repeat themselves frequently?

- Does the number of requests and explanations keep growing?
- Do they preach over and over again?
- Do they try to speak in a piercing or emphatic tone in order to make an impression?
- Does it look as if their children enjoy the argument itself, try to draw the parents into an argument, or use arguments to weaken their parents' position?

These are all signs that the parents are being swept away in the waves of verbiage and thereby losing their influence and sense of presence.

Am I drawn into threats, shouting and impulsive reactions?

Many parents feel that a sharp and immediate reaction to the child's problem behavior or provocations is necessary or else they will look weak and lose face. They feel such a response is necessary in order for their children to get their message. Here are some statements made by parents that illustrate this point:

- I give as good as I get!
- Does he think he's gonna scare me with threats? I will give him a reason to be afraid!
- I have to show her once and for all!
- If I don't answer, he'll think he won!

These statements indicate that the parents are trapped in the feeling they have no choice but to respond instantly and strongly to every provocation or problem behavior. They feel any other reaction proves they lost the fight. These statements reveal a problematic expectation: the hope that if a reaction is strong enough, a child will learn once and for all. This hope almost never comes true. In almost all cases, shouts, threats, and raging outbursts lead to escalation of tension and loss of parents' influence. Parents do not control these events but get sucked into a vortex that swallows up their parenthood.

The erosion of parenthood in a storm of shouts, scolds and empty threats is obvious, for example, in the case of parents of restless children who are currently characterized as suffering from ADHD. The parents of such children find themselves turning on a merry-go-round with the permanent background grind of phrases like "Stop it!" "No!" "I told you so!" "If you don't stop, I'll..." and so on and so forth. No wonder at the end of the day the parent feels exhausted, a condition that can be referred to as "hassled parent." The hassled parent feels tossed this way and that, pulled and pushed, and loses the feeling that he or she is running the show. In order to evaluate such situations, my colleagues and I created the *Hassled Parent Questionnaire*. Our studies, based on the results of this questionnarie, have showed two very important findings:[1]

- parents of children with ADHD are much more hassled than other parents; and
- with training, parents can get off the merry-go-round and restore their authority and influence with their children.

Parents often complain that their child doesn't hear, doesn't listen or ignores them. Parents who feel the need to repeat the same thing many times or to raise their voices in order to penetrate their child's awareness do not understand the mechanism of habituation built into our nervous systems. This mechanism leads us to automatically stop hearing constant noises. The voices of parents who repeat themselves, scold, shout, and constantly comment on their children's behavior are catalogued by the child's brain as "background noise." This begins a process of habituation such that the child's nervous system responds less and less to the parent's voice. Paradoxically, the parent's very attempt to penetrate the wall of disregard by repetition and increasing the volume strengthens the habituation mechanism. The feeling of these parents that the more they scold the less the child hears is correct even on the physiological level: the signals of neural reception of the parental speech in the child's brain become weaker and weaker. Actually, parents mute their voices through a constant droning of requests, scoldings, and shouts.

---

1 I've been helped all along by teams conducting projects and research in various countries. A short and simple description of those studies can be found in https://www.haimomer-nvr.com/

A different process happens to parents who try to show their child once and for all that she or he cannot continue with her or his problematic ways. A case in point is a father who grounds his son or bans television for an entire month. Often, one parent is more likely to impose a punishment and expect the other parent to enforce it. No wonder these punishments are rarely carried out and become another step in the process of parental erosion. The result is even more serious: the father is angry at the mother for not carrying out his punishment and the mother is angry at the father for putting the burden on her shoulders. The gap between the parents grows and their parental weight drops accordingly. Often the father responds by demonstratively giving up ("If they don't do it my way, they can manage without me!") and thereby only deepens his marginality in the family. Sometimes the damage of sharp punishments is even greater, especially when the child in question is particularly rebellious. These children never surrender. They feel surrender is like annihilation. In their mind, if they bow their heads they will be erased. Such children wage an all-out war against any attempt to subdue them. And if they do supposedly bow their heads, they do so only tactically, while promising themselves to pay back their parents for the humiliation.

Do I give up my space, my leisure and my goals for my child?

Many parents get caught in such situations out of deep concern for their children. They are aware of the price they pay in their personal space, careers, leisure and intimate relationships. But they feel they have no choice because otherwise they will cause their child deep suffering. Sometimes their emotional identification with the child is so great that the child's suffering fills their whole world. They no longer have independent feelings but always feel as a function of their child's emotional state.

Accommodation and Self-Sacrifice

The answers to the questions below can provide insights into whether a parent is being too self-sacrificing.

- My child sleeps in our bed because he can't sleep alone. He also has severe separation anxiety. We can't spend any time alone and a couple's vacation is out of the question!
- My teenage daughter will not let me invite over two of my girlfriends she hates.

- I gave up my job because I understood my son needs me all the time!

A handicapped child or a severely sick child puts their parents to ultimate tests of devotion. No wonder parents who are willing to sacrifice to support their child draw deep respect. However, when the child's emotional difficulties lead the parent to accommodate themselves and their entire life routine to spare the child pain, stress or anxiety, the results can be the opposite of the expected. Thus, instead of the child being less anxious, they become more anxious and less functional. Instead of the parent being the strong support who steadies their child in overcoming their problems, the parent's guiding role is erased, and the parent becomes an instrument of the child's avoidance and recalcitrance.

Evidence from an ever increasing amount of research confirms the damage that constant *parental accommodation* causes to children's independent functioning. The term, *parental accommodation,* indicates a process in which parents become pliable and change their ways so that their child will not suffer or in order to earn a little "peace and quiet." As for anxiety disorders, whether social anxiety, separation anxiety, specific phobias, obsessive-compulsive disorder (OCD) or post-traumatic stress disorder (PTSD), parental accommodation to the child's demands or expectations has proven to lead to a worsening of the problem.. Accommodation is also the decisive factor in the success or failure of therapy, whether psychological or pharmaceutical. Thus, when parents demonstrate high levels of accommodation, the chances for success of their child's treatment drop significantly. This is true even for pharmaceutical treatments! In contrast, systematic coaching of parents to reduce accommodation achieves improvement both in anxiety levels and in functioning.

Studies have found a significant undermining of functioning not only in the case of anxiety disorders but also for parental accommodation in other situations as well. One of the striking discoveries had to do with infant sleeping difficulties. When parents rush to soothe their infant, take him out of bed, hold him, or alternatively, lie down with him until he falls asleep, they cause sleeping problems to increase.

When parents constantly and instantly rush to soothe their baby, they actually prevent the baby from developing the ability to self-soothe. Thus, both for anxious children and babies with sleeping problems, when parents are "infected" with the child's distress, they stop providing the correct support, which enables the child to develop his or her abilities.

The problematic consequences of erosion of parental authority and parental accommodation continue throughout the child's life. Thus, parental capitulation to expectations and demands that are not connected with the child's willingness to make efforts to cope, increase the risk of the development of *entitled dependency* in adolescents and adult children. This syndrome is characterized by refusal and withdrawal from school and work and sometimes also social withdrawal and long self-isolation at home. Here, too, the parents get swept away by their child's functioning difficulties and signs of distress and broadly shield their child against the demands of the outside world. When this happens, the adult child is provided a "degenerative shelter," a parental umbrella that protects against pressures but guarantees continued personal dysfunction and decline. The program we developed to help parents reduce their accommodation and regain their sense of impact and initiative in cases of entitled dependency has led to a significant improvement both in parents' ability to defend themselves against the demands of their child and in the ability of the child, once grown, to function as an adult.

Personal Space and Boundaries

The following questions about loss of personal space and boundaries will help parents find out whether and to what degree they are giving positive support or pernicious protection:

- Has my time stopped being my own and actually become my child's time because of his or her anxiety or difficulties? (For instance, cutting into my work or leisure activities).

- Has my personal space been limited by my child's difficulties? (For instance, the child is sleeping in the parental bed or has unlimited access to the parents' personal space or belongings).

- Do I feel overwhelmed and need to respond immediately to prevent or instantly stop my child's distress?

- Are the family's daily life and routine dictated by my child's anxieties, difficulties or demands? (For instance, do I perform more and more actions instead of the child? Or, are special habits evolving in the house that are meant solely to satisfy my child's needs or ease his or her distress?)
- Am I capable of preventing my child from interrupting me in conversations or personal activities?
- Do I have the right to my own wishes and plans? Am I able to realize those wishes and plans?

Many parents are metaphorically erased in a gradual process of inadvertently losing their place, voice, and will to exigencies of the child's distress, expectations, and demands. Sometimes, the parental loss is a voluntary sacrifice, and sometimes it is forced. Sometimes, the child threatens severe reactions if the parents do not cooperate. Other times, the child's very suffering and distress are so unbearable for parents that they feel compelled to give in to the child's demands. In all of these cases, the result is the same: the parents lose themselves and their impact whereas the child loses his or her self-esteem and ability to function.

Am I becoming marginalized and know increasingly less about my child?

Samantha: I don't know who my daughter's friends are. When they visit, she purposely makes it impossible for me to communicate with them.

Richard: When I ask where he's going, he gives general answers like "out with friends," and will not elaborate. There have been cases where he said he was going to a certain friend's house but it turned out he was not there.

Laura: When my son sits at the computer, he locks the door. His best friend is his cell phone!

Robert: I feel alien to my children's world!

Martha: When I want to know something, I prefer to spy behind her back. That allows me to find things out without a confrontation.

The Influence of Technology

Many parents feel as if their child is living in a world that has become increasingly alien and closed to them. The feeling of marginalization is particularly stark as a result of the speed of technological changes. Today's children are growing up in a completely different world from the one their parents grew up in. Cell phones, social networks and online games have created an almost impermeable alternative reality. When a child sinks into the virtual world, having even a simple conversation or making eye contact is difficult. The amount of mutually attentive time parents spend with their children is decreasing. Much has been said about the impact of the digital world on child development, but the fact that the child is lost in his or her cell phone has just as much impact on parental development, with parents being "trained" to be marginal players in their child's life from an early age. They learn to step aside and allow themselves to be excluded from any meaningful discourse in which their child is engaged. As a result, their child considers their parents' appeals a nuisance. Many parents try to go with the flow and do not realize that they are allowing limitations on their parental role. If they do dare to do something about the cell phone, it is to threaten to punish the child by taking it away when the child misbehaves. This threat can escalate arguments and lead to further erosion of their impact as parents. How to handle the use of a cell phone within the family becomes a major challenge for every parent.

The Place of Privacy

Another change that pushes parents to the margins is the sanctity of privacy, which has today become not just one important value among other values but rather a supreme value that must not be questioned under any circumstances. We call this sweeping and automatic position the "privacy reflex." Adolescents today will blame their parents for violating their privacy with a feeling of righteous indignation even when it is clear they are using their privacy in a harmful way. The protest is vocal and effective for several reasons:

- The child is filled with a sense of justice when waving the flag of his or her privacy;
- Parents shrink at that accusation of invasion of privacy; and
- Today's social milieu reinforces the right to privacy, often rebuking the parents for infringing it.

As the areas in which privacy is considered a right expand, in inverse proportion parents' impact shrinks. Areas of life considered private and off-limits to parents include the child's room, belongings, money, friends, leisure activities, and, of course, the cell phone.

Parents cherish privacy and discretion as untouchable values even though in many cases the child is clearly at risk. Holding to these values may then deepen their helplessness in supervising their children and increases their marginality in their children's lives. In the name of discretion and privacy, parents put themselves into a position of being isolated and unsupported. When the child's demands for privacy meet the parents' total respect for discretion, parents' influence evaporates, establishing a deadly equation guaranteed to produce parental paralysis:

Absolute privacy of the child + absolute parental discretion = zero influence.

Sometimes, parents try to circumvent the privacy and discretion trap by spying. Parents who spy gain an illusion of control but are actually deepening their helplessness and polluting their relationship with the child by lying. The helplessness increases because the parent cannot act on the basis of knowledge they collected behind the child's back unless the action is also performed secretly. Sometimes, this situation pushes parents into complicated and risky schemes when they try to act following a discovery that was made illegitimately. One father who discovered his daughter smoked grass with her boyfriend in the house took this to the extreme: in order not to expose that he had searched his daughter's room, he conspired with a friend who was a police investigator. The investigator approached the daughter and told her confidentially that the police drug unit was following her and her boyfriend. The girl promised she would stop but made the police officer swear not to tell her father. The investigator friend agreed. This supposedly solved the problem, but the creation of a fake relationship between the father's friend and the daughter, ostensibly in order to hide from the father something that he had actually discovered himself, actually weakened the father's influence.

Extent of Disconnectedness

For parents to find out for themselves to what degree they have become marginal and disconnected and to what degree they are trapped in a bubble of helplessness, they can ask themselves the following questions:

- Is it hard for me to reach my children because they are lost in the computer or cell phone?
- Do I know who my children's friends are and what their leisure activities are?
- Do I know how they are doing at school?
- Will I get answers to questions that I ask?
- Do my children throw a fit when they think I am violating their privacy?
- Am I afraid to openly check what they are doing in areas where they might be getting into trouble?
- Do I try to hide the reason for my interest and try to elicit information without them feeling I'm doing it?
- Do I feel I have become a marginal factor in their lives?

With these questions, parents can evaluate to what extent their presence has been harmed. The undermining of parental vigilance is a destructive process because parental vigilant care is the primary way to prevent the child from doing dangerous things. The combination of lack of vigilance, proliferation of temptations for children, and the anonymity of the modern world creates an explosive environment in which children are exposed to greater danger at the same time that parents are being kept out of their lives.

The Anchoring Parent

The answer to drifting, marginalization, and loss of influence is for parents to stand firm and be anchors for their children. An anchor stabilizes a ship by firmly attaching it to the ground. Thus, for parents to become anchors for their children, they must firmly attach their children to their "parental ground." Anchoring the child begins with self-anchoring. If parents do not stabilize themselves in their role as parents, they will not be able to stop the drifting but rather will be torn away or swept away by the currents that suck up their child. Parental anchoring is based on four pillars: presence, self-control, support, and structure.

Presence

The anchoring parent has a palpable presence. The parent's influence cannot be canceled out or chased away. Children experience their parents as present when their parents send them the message, "I am your parent! You cannot fire me, divorce me, or silence me! I am here, and I am staying here!" When parents behave in a way that conveys presence, children feel they have parents and not just suppliers of money and services. Parents, too, feel themselves as present, that they have a voice, impact, and influence. With their determined presence, parents lay the foundation for stability in the family. Parental presence is not expressed by an angry or authoritarian outburst but by firmness and consistency. The expression of presence is the opposite of impulsive outrage. The message "I am here and I am staying here!" creates the condition that even when children are not aware of it, even when they are with their friends or busy on social networks, the parental anchor is there in the depths.

Aidy (13) was a precocious and independent girl. Her father Maury, with whom she lived, had remarried. Aidy's relationship with her father and his new wife fluctuated between periods of closeness and periods of coldness and hostility. In the bad times, she stayed away for many hours and even spent a few nights sleeping at a girlfriends' house. Maury felt Aidy was not only independent but also responsible so he avoided taking a clear stance on when and under what conditions she could stay with her girlfriend, especially because usually after a few such days she would come home in a friendly mood.

This changed when Maury found out that Aidy had been cutting school and starting avoiding answering his questions. When he pressed her, she threatened she would move to her mother's. Even though the threat was not very realistic because the court had given him custody of Aidy, it still shook his confidence. In a conversation with the school advisor, Maury said he avoided taking on an authoritative attitude with Aidy in order to maintain harmony and prevent a deterioration in the relationship. Maury admitted that Aidy's threat to move in with her mother had shaken his confidence. The advisor told him: "I think Aidy keeps you under a constant threat of being 'fired.' She makes you feel like you are a parent on probation, but that only worsens her feeling of being a driven leaf. But actually, Aidy cannot fire you!"

The advisor had hit the right spot. Even while they were talking, Maury started to regain his footing as a father.

The next day Maury contacted some of Aidy's friends' mothers and asked them to let him know every time Aidy came over. He also agreed with Aidy's homeroom teacher that if Aidy cut class the teacher was to inform him immediately.

After that, Maury sat Aidy down for a talk and said, "For the last few months, I felt you were drifting to bad places. At first, I didn't react because I thought if I went along with you you would come to your senses. Now I understand that that wasn't good for you or for me. Since you've been cutting school and disappearing, I have decided to watch over you closely. I'm in touch with your friends' parents and in daily contact with school. If you cut class, I will look for you. If you sleep at a friend's house, I will talk to her parents and, if necessary, I will go there. I am your father, and I will be your father come hell or high water. You are too important to me for me to give up on you!"

Maury felt that every one of the contacts he had made and every visit to the school sent a message of presence: "I am here! I am here! I am here!" He did not act aggressively, did not threaten, and did not speak in an authoritarian tone. On the contrary, he spoke only from love and devotion. Aidy did not answer him but within a week her behavior stabilized. Her father's standing firm enabled her to stop living like a dry leaf that was blown by the wind of every new whim or influence.

Self-control

The development of self-control enables parents to withstand daily challenges and unusual situations. Contrary to the view that self-control is an in-born personal trait, many studies prove that parents can develop skills to enable them to overcome their impulsive reactions and take a much firmer stand than they ever thought was possible. It turns out that "self-control muscles" can be strengthened just as much as any other muscle. In our parent-training programs, we coined three phrases that illustrate the principles of self-control:

1. Strike while the iron is cold![2]

2. You don't need to win, just to persist!

3. Mistakes are inevitable, but they can be corrected!

When parents understand these principles and first start applying them, they discover that previously explosive situations become manageable.

Rita spent a lot of time alone with her son (Tom, 8), partly because his father, a high-tech specialst, worked long hours and often traveled for work. Rita had managed this situation well with her three older children, but Tom seriously pushed her limits. He was clingy and demanding. When he demanded she buy him something, he would repeat his demand in an increasingly shriller voice. If Rita did not acquiesce, he would throw a raging temper tantrum.

Rita was exhausted. Sometimes she gave in to Tom just to get some peace and quiet. She said his voice penetrated her ears and pierced her head like a drill. She started to suffer from migraines, which

2 Irvin Yalom, a professor at Stanford Universtiy, proposed this re-stating of the well-known idiom, strike *while the iron is hot*, to emphasize the need to act with deliberation, not impulse, for best results.

made her even more sensitive to noise. Every cry and demand by Tom became a serious challenge for her. She started to cringe as soon as she heard the special tone of voice that signaled a new demand.

She shared her situation with a friend who had two children with ADHD. Her friend, who had received parent coaching according to our plan, offered Rita a simple and surprising way to expand her sense of mental space and improve her feeling of control in the face of Tom's nagging. The idea was to combine the principle of delayed action (strike while the iron is cold), with a tangible means of self-defense (actually, protection of her ears).

Following that conversation, Rita told Tom that every time he asked her to buy something for him she would answer him the next day. She showed him she was writing the request down in a special notebook and noting the date and time the request was made.

Of course, Tom did not change his conduct following his mother's announcement. He launched right into his habit of clingy nagging and vocal attrition. Now the mother brought in the second measure: she put on earplugs and said to him, "I'm putting in earplugs because then I won't get angry when you shout! I can still hear you but softer and then I don't get mad!" To show Tom that the earplugs lowered the volume of his voice coming in her ears but she could still hear him, she put the earplugs in him and talked to him, so that he could hear her voice, although muffled. She also practiced making a calm, almost indifferent facial expression as if she were hypnotized.

Tom did not become a quiet child following the intervention, but Rita gained the sense that she had better self-control. She surrendered much less and also stopped her angry outbursts. Tom's nagging demanding went down to much more reasonable levels. Rita, in the meantime, felt that she had regained not only her place as a mother but also her ears.

Support

A relatively small anchor can stabilize a large ship thanks to the three hooks it sinks into the ground. Likewise, a parent who knows how to share with relatives and close friends, and get their support can become an anchor for their child in a way that might have been impossible if they had acted alone.

Joining with family members, friends, or the school for consistent action is not easy for many parents. The need for privacy and the conviction that all concerned should solve their problems by themselves makes it difficult to ask for support. However, parents who overcome this barrier discover that they develop broad shoulders, and the help of supporters gives them legitimacy, influence, and stability.

Many parents think they do not have meaningful supporters and therefore are doomed to act on their own. These parents are not aware that they are automatically ruling out relevant support options. Thinking that "Grandmother is sick—I don't want to bother her," "everyone is busy with his or her own business—people don't have time to help," "we don't have supporters—we live far away from our family," and "I am too ashamed to ask" seal parents in a private bubble and block every initiative for seeking help. But, "support muscles" can be trained and strengthened. The following examples point to the tremendous possibilities for self-stabilization and parental anchoring inherent in the correct appeal for help.

Hugo (14) hit his sister Shirley (11) and humiliated her in front of her friends. Their mother heard the shouting, went into the room, ordered Hugo to get out, saying she would consider her next steps. In the past, the mother would respond by shouting, making threats, and giving punishments, which didn't help: Hugo would just return to harass his sister, and the mother would once more lose control.

This time the mother decided to act differently. A few hours after the next incident, Hugo got a phone call from his grandfather in New York, who said, "You know you are very precious to me, and I think the world of you. But what you did to your sister today is terrible, and you have to completely stop it. If you're angry, you can call me right away, and we'll find a way to calm down and solve the problem. But hitting, spitting, and insulting, like you did today, are absolutely wrong. I will continue to be in the picture. As I'm sure you remember, your sister is just as much my beloved grandchild as you are!"

Hugo asked his grandfather if his mother had told him what happened. His grandfather said: "You bet she did! I knew there were problems, and now I just ask about it every time!"

Later that day Hugo got an email from his aunt in Moscow. His aunt expressed similar thoughts to his grandfather. Hugo went to his mother and asked with astonishment: "Does the whole world know what happened between me and Shirley?"

The mother said: "If you insult or hit her, the whole world will know!"

In the following weeks Hugo's grandfather talked to him a few times and every time expressed his appreciation for his self-control.

***

Ozzie (12) was a restless child who was easily pulled into bad company. He was caught with two friends trying to light a fire with toilet paper rolls in the school trash can. They were suspended for three days.

At the end of the suspension, the principal met with each one of the three children and their parents. He told them that there was still a missing link needed to resolve the affair: The children must find a way to perform an act of reparation for the school, which would restore their status as students in good standing with full rights and responsibilities. He explained, "There is a principle in our society that 'if you break it, you have to fix it.' The school needs you to perform an act of good will to fix what you broke in your relationship with the school by your vandalism. You don't have to offer me anything right now. I'm waiting for a joint proposal in three days" He asked if there were any questions and ended the meeting.

On the way home, Ozzie started talking to his parents about a possible action to repair his standing with the school. After talking with his friends, though, Ozzie changed his mind and expressed anger and resentment. He said he learned that anyone who has served a punishment is considered innocent because the punishment erases the action. He claimed the principal just wanted to humiliate them. It was clear that Ozzie was parroting his friends.

His parents saw this as an opportunity to help Ozzie stop tagging along with others. They told him they would think about it but that reparation had to be made to the school because they agreed with the principal.

The next day Ozzie received an unexpected visit from his cousin Dave, whom he admired, partly because at 22 he was making a good living as a professional soccer player and had already won two titles. Dave told him, "I heard about the fire, the suspension, and the principal's demand for reparation. I understand your anger because they didn't talk to you about reparation but just suspended you. I want to help you get out of this tight spot. I know your parents are determined to comply with the demand for compensation, and I actually understand them. Such an action will restore the family honor. The question is how to do it so that you also feel it is honorable and that you don't feel humiliated by complying!"

The two thought it over, and Dave suggested an idea that Ozzie thought was very respectful: the parents of each one of the children would donate a soccer ball to the school, with each of the children chipping in by donating part of their allowance. With Dave's help, they would organize a special sports event featuring a game between two seventh grade classes.

Dave talked to Ozzie's parents and then to the parents of the other two children. Dave, whose name was also familiar to Ozzie's two friends, told them: "If you do it, you will get out of this honorably. Everybody will respect you! I will be the referee in the game between the seventh grades."

At the opening of the festive game, the principal announced to all the participants that he appreciated the three children and their families for the way they managed to right a wrong and contribute to the whole school community. Everyone cheered and clapped.

Rules, Routine and Structure

In a household characterized by a lack of rules, binding routine, or clear assignation of responsibilities, stopping deterioration in the parent-child relationship is very difficult. Parents and children alike find nothing to hold on to. How do you start creating order and structure when you are used to everything being vague and fluid? Many parents who followed our program were surprised to discover that order is a process that expands and spreads the moment you create a clear core that allows it to grow. It is like the formation of crystals in a liquid solution; sometimes, it suffices to introduce an initial crystallizing element for the liquid matter to start arranging itself, attaching, and forming a structure. Sometimes, the initial spark that sets the whole process in motion is the parents drawing a red line concerning one unacceptable behavior. The parents decide and announce the unacceptable behavior they are going to resist firmly. Following their announcement they act resolutely to carry out the first "no," the constitutional "no" of their parenthood. Gradually, the parents become more and more able to live up to statements such as: "It is our house!" "In our house, we sit down to meals together!" "In our house, screens go off at 11 PM!"

For years the Levy family believed in spontaneity and freedom in child-rearing. The parents believed that each child is born with a core of unique selfhood, and that only under conditions of free growth, without restraints or demands, could that core develop optimally. The atmosphere at home was harmonious and positive.

The difficulties appeared only with the third child, Ron, who from a young age showed a tendency to seclude himself from the family and spend all his free time in his room. His parents respected his tendencies and independence. Even when they noticed with pain that Ron preferred to stay alone and not join family gatherings, they stayed loyal to their principles and let him do as he wished. Ron also preferred to eat alone in front of the TV and started to miss more family meals. In adolescence, Ron started taking his food to his room. Further, Ron started to be late for school and sometimes preferred to stay home the whole day. His grades were declining. Getting ready for school in the morning got infinitely harder, and the mother, who was responsible for getting the children ready and sending them off, felt overwhelmed and started screaming at them. Gradually, freedom started to look like anarchy.

Following repeated complaints from school about Ron's tardiness and absences, the parents decided it was time to take action. Under the guidance of the school psychologist, they decided to make a joint announcement to their three children. They gathered them all in the living room and informed them, "We have decided to change the household rules. From now on, no more eating in your rooms or in front of the TV. We are going to stand firmly against those habits. We are going to eat breakfast and dinner together at the table. To make sure everybody gets out of the house on time, breakfast will be ready and on the table by 7:15!"

The parents surprised themselves when they made this decision. At first, it didn't even sound like their own voices. The children were also skeptical. Before bed, the parents sat with Ron to prepare his school bag and clothes so everything would be ready in the morning. They got up half an hour earlier, made breakfast, and woke up the kids. The father's involvement enabled Ron to get to the table on time, washed and dressed. It was the first family breakfast in a long time. Breakfast and getting out to school became the core activity of the new order, which gradually spread to other life areas. The parents felt strengthened and on the following days began enforcing the rule of no eating in bedrooms or in front of the TV. Ron's isolation tendencies did not disappear, but he was no longer eating in his room or missing meals. He stopped cutting school. The parents still gave their children a lot of freedom, but they made sure personal space did not come at the expense of the family. Family meals became just as sacred as the principle of spontaneity.

Love and Parental Anchoring

The title of one of the best known books ever written about parenting is *Love Is Not Enough*[3]. We all know that love is an essential element of both emotional and physical development. One of the most important

3 Bettelheim, B. (1950) *Love is not enough: the treatment of emotionally disturbed children* Glencoe IL: Free Press

studies of infant development showed that children raised in institutions in conditions of emotional neglect and lack of touch suffer from severe emotional and physical damage. A loving parent is like a safe harbor: that parent gives children the feeling they can always find relief, encouragement and comfort in the parent's embrace. Loving parents provide their children with the emotional security that allows them to embark on exploring the world around them, to play, to learn and to develop their independence. These are the basic conditions of *secure attachment,* i.e., the emotional security that gives the developing child a sense of self-worth and the ability to attach to others.

For a child to develop secure attachment, love is not enough. The parent needs to be not only loving but also strong enough to stabilize the child and protect him or her against the dangers of the environment and the child's internal impulses. A safe harbor is not limited to an embracing, accepting, and encouraging attitude. The harbor will be safe only if the ship is anchored. The parental anchor stabilizes and protects the developing child from being carried away by the currents, tempted by the song of the Sirens, or harmed by the surging impulses from within. Without an anchor, there is no secure attachment. Parental anchoring is the element of strength that adds to love the necessary element of stability.

The combination of love and strength is also biologically critical because children are vulnerable creatures. Throughout infancy and childhood, children can only survive by attaching to a strong adult figure who is able to protect them and prepare them to deal with life's challenges. One of the important conclusions from this insight is that if the parent is not strong enough to provide stability and protection, the love the parent gives becomes de-valued because the child will not experience a sense of protection and security. Thus, the love of a weak parent sometimes becomes despised love. This process is cruelly illustrated by the following example:

> *Alex (15) was once his mother's darling. Their special closeness was expressed in countless ways. His mother kissed, hugged, and petted him, and Alex felt special and beloved. He even talked to his mother in a sort of private language. His mother had a heavy Polish accent, and her English was full of mistakes. When Alex talked to her, he naturally mimicked her accent and mistakes. He wasn't*

mocking her but doing it out of love to create a special closeness with her.

When Alex reached puberty he started blatantly rejecting his mother. He stopped using his special way of talking to her, distanced himself from her, made choices opposite to her taste, and refused all physical contact, no matter how small. He would insult his mother and actively deride her.

His mother suffered deeply from his rejection. She cried, begged, and sunk into depression. Her severe state not only failed to draw her son closer but also actually deepened his aversion to her. Once she expressed to him in tears her deep sense of his betrayal, saying, "You used to be a loving son! Now I feel like a garbage can! When I try to kiss you, I feel I actually disgust you!"

Alex replied with cruel frankness, "Who wants to be kissed by a garbage can?"

Everyone understands that forms of endearment suitable for a little boy are not suitable for an adolescent. Even so, similar examples of rejection and derision of parental love can also appear in much younger children. Parents ask with astonishment, "Where did you learn that? We don't behave that way in our house!" It is not hard to find the answer: the child copies ways of speech and behavior from others whom he experiences as strong. In trying to resemble them, he gives his parents the message: "I don't want to belong to those who are weak!" Parents' challenge in these cases is not to show the child more love but rather more determination to defend themselves and him against destructive impulses and a problematic society. What is needed is not the gentleness of an accepting embrace, but the strength and tenacity of a parental anchor.

Conclusion

The challenges to parents today differ from those in the past. The reason has to do both with changes in the structure of society and changes in values and beliefs about child rearing. The salient social changes are the weakening of the extended family and high rate of divorced and single parents, the growth of cities with their infinite temptations, and the growth of the Internet and cell phones that expose children to a bombardment of influences never seen before. At the same time, lack of clarity about the parental role has taken root. Whereas in the past parents had to take care of their children's physical needs and give them basic concepts of right and wrong, today the parental job is much vaguer. The result is a generation of "confused parents," who are often dismayed and weak in the face of the erosion of the relatonship between them and their children.

Review and Application

- Ask yourself whether you tend to chatter, preach and over-explain.
- Ask yourself whether you are drawn into pointless confrontations with your child.
- Ask yourself whether your personal space, leisure time and intimate relationship have suffered because of your children's anxieties or difficulties.
- Ask yourself whether you know less and less about what is happening in areas where your child might get into trouble.
- Ask yourself whether the smartphone and computer have taken over your children's lives to the point that you have become marginal.
- The optimal answer to these challenges is the parental anchoring function. Parents who serve as anchors stabilize their children against the drift and give them security and belonging.
- The role of the anchor is based on resolute presence. Learn to give the message with your actions: "I am your parent! You cannot fire me, divorce me or silence me! I am here to stay!"
- The role of the anchor is based on self-control. Learn to break free from being drawn into conflict and escalation.

- The role of the anchor is based on support from the environment. Learn how to develop broad shoulders and speak to the child in the language of "we."
- The role of the anchor is based on stable rules that provide clear order and structure in the life of the child and the family.

Chapter Two

Self-control

Our studies[4] have proven that increasing parents' self-control can play a key role in raising their status and improving the child's problems. In this chapter, we will present a series of take-away lessons and steps parents can apply to overcome their impulsive reactions and develop judgment, patience and persistence. We will learn how these changes transform the relationship between the parent and the child and arm the parent with strength, stability and influence.

I cannot control you; I can only control myself!

This insight is one of the keys to improving the mutual relationship between parents and children of all ages. Whereas when children are small their parents must physically stop them from making dangerous or destructive moves, the older the child gets the harder it gets. The truth is that from early childhood parents are not really in control. Parents find out quickly they cannot control their children's thoughts and feelings. They gradually understand that it is difficult to control their child's behavior, too. For example, parents might discover their children do the opposite of what they want, "just to spite them." This reaction indicates the development of the child's autonomous will and natural aversion to coercion. Parents who try to overpower their children's protests and force them to behave as they wish find out that the moment their children are

4 Gershy, N., Meehan, K. B., Omer, H., Papouchis, N., & Schorr-Sapir, I. (2017). Randomized Clinical Trial of Mindfulness Skills Augmentation in Parent Training. *Child Youth Care Forum, 46* (6), 783-803.

not near them they behave contrary to their demands. This inclination gets stronger with age, and parents' attempts to control adolescents in particular can lead to a result opposite of the one desired.

Fortunately, there is a good alternative to attempts to control a child: a combination of personal example, reasonable explanation, and standing firm. Standing firm is not the same as trying to control. When parents present a firm stance, they are exercising their control over themselves, not over their child. The parent is not saying to the child "you will do what I say!" but rather "I will do what I say!"

The moral basis of standing firm is the parent's sense of duty. Unfortunately, today many parents have lost the ability to say "it is my duty!" in a clear and determined voice. The phrase "it is my duty!" grates on the ears of many parents. *Duty* has become an unpopular, stuffy, tinny word, like the grating voice of an old-fashioned schoolmarm. Many parents prefer to rely on persuasion, rewards or even seduction. But what should they do when their child is not convinced? Or when the very attempt to convince turns into an endless discussion? To stop these dynamics, parents need to take a clear stand that cannot be shaken by questions, tricks, or protests. Their basis for doing this is the sense of duty that reflects their concern and responsibility for their child. Just as you need axioms that cannot be questioned in mathematics, the same goes for parenting. Parents' duty is the "axiom" upon which healthy and stable relations with children are built. Parents whose sense of duty is vague or who are hesitant about doing their duty prevent their children from experiencing stability. When that happens, the familial ship rocks about without an anchor.

By saying "it is my duty!" the parent invites a very different interaction than by saying "you will do as I say!" Since children naturally seek autonomy, the message "you will do as I say!" clashes with an inner drive. Many children react as if they were allergic to having orders and warnings leveled at them. No wonder certain parents feel as if their children enjoy disobeying them! Indeed, children enjoy discovering they have an independent will that their parents cannot bend.

From a young age, children who resist their parents's wishes exhibit three typical reactions:

- impudence;
- indifference; and

- internal rage.

Impudence is an overt and explicit resistance that expresses a defiant rejection of the parents' wishes. For instance, the child may scream at the parent or shrug his or her shoulders in a show of defiance.

Indifference is a sophisticated form of resistance expressed by the parents' words washing over the child without leaving a mark. For example, the child ignores the parents' demands without saying a word, possibly just rolling his or her eyes in a quiet show of derision.

The harshest reaction is that of children who respond to their parents by turning their gaze inward, puckering their lips and stiffening their necks. These physical responses indicate growing rage and determination to act in a way that defies the parents' will or even seeks revenge on them for trying to impose it. When you convey to a child the message "you must do what I say," you give them only two choices: obedience or rebellion. Children who refuse to obey are necessarily pushed into the other option. It is very different when the parent conveys the message: "It is my duty to take care of you!" This presents the child with a third option: cooperation. This is a positive option that is completely different from obedience.

Moira, the mother of Liz (13), fought with her daughter every day over homework, but Liz was glued to the social networks. Moira explained, shouted, threatened, and punished. She withheld Liz's allowance and grounded her to no avail. When Moira tried to turn the computer off while Liz was sitting in front of it, Liz reacted violently.

When Liz's parents came to the parent-coaching program, Moira was completely exhausted by the incessant fights and Liz's complete refusal of any request or demand. The program's first order of business was to restore Moira's sense of self-control. Moira learned how to contain herself and delay her reaction in the face of her daughter's provocations. The father, Ronnie, came into the picture to display a firm stance together with Moira.

The parents went into Liz's room and said, "We realize you cannot be controlled. We cannot control your mouth, your hands, or your legs. But we can control ourselves, and it is our duty not to supply you with things that harm you. The free surfing we provide you with has become a source of harm for you. We must not give you something that destroys you!"

After that statement, they left her room. Two days later, Liz was surprised to discover that her surfing account was blocked and the modem in her room had been taken away. Liz could still surf at her friends' houses or sometimes on her brother's computer, but surfing via these options was limited and inconvenient. Liz protested, threatened, and cried, but her parents, who had been coached on how to withstand her pressure, kept their word.

A few days later, Nancy, a family friend who had a good relationship with Liz, entered the picture. She told Liz she wanted to find a cooperative solution that kept Liz's dignity intact but also allowed her to function. At first, Liz was not interested. Nancy called her a few days later and emphasized the matter of saving her dignity. This time Liz agreed. The very mention of saving her dignity gave her the feeling there might be a third option besides surrender or rebellion.

Nancy suggested Liz come over to her house for a few days after school both to reduce the tension at home and also to catch up on schoolwork. This enabled Liz to experience a kind of cooperation that did not feel like defeated surrender to her parents' terms. A few days later, her mother told her, "We're proud of you! We see your initiative to catch up on schoolwork with Nancy as an important step!"

Ronnie agreed with Liz on two measures: (1) restoring her surfing and computer and (2) having a short phone call with her every afternoon at four. He put the phone call on his schedule so that it had the status of a work appointment. Ronnie would ask about her homework but also give Liz the opportunity to plan her day. This enabled Liz to feel she could cooperate with a sense of dignity.

For a while, Liz preferred to do her homework at Nancy's, even on days when Nancy was not home. After a while, she started doing homework at home. Moira, meanwhile, improved her ability to withstand provocations without reacting belligerently. The relationship between Moira and Liz got better. Confrontations lessened and Moira felt she could now again initiate joint activities that used to be enjoyable for both of them.

To establish cooperation with a rebellious child, the parents must overcome their feelings of helplessness and their lack of self-control and look for solutions that maintain the child's dignity. Given these conditions, cooperation can grow although it usually happens gradually because the child wishes to show that he or she decided to cooperate out of choice rather than blind obedience.

Even though giving up the illusion of control produces positive results for the child and parents, some parents find it hard to do. They believe that if the child does not surrender, it means they are weak. These parents say "he'll think he won!" The fear of being weak runs deep in the human psyche and has both biological and cultural roots. Throughout evolution and history, the strong-weak dichotomy has been experienced existentially: the weak were slated for extinction. It is important to understand the depth of the wish for power in the simple and literal sense of the word so that we can offer parents a convincing alternative, namely power based on self-control, standing firm, persistence, and legitimacy.

Some parents (typically fathers) respond to the demand to develop self-control by asking, "So, when he curses me, am I supposed to just sit there?" or, "Am I supposed to let her walk all over me?"

We do not disregard the question of power but address it honestly. We say, "You must be much stronger than you are today, but strong in a different way that gives you back your stability, firmness and status. If you show self-control and determination, your son will feel you are a solid rock!" Perhaps the "rock" image will not be attractive to many parents. We would then say : "When your child pulls with all their strength, you can be as strong as an anchor!

The principle of Delayed Action: Strike while the iron is cold!

We all know that to control ourselves in moments of anger we must prevent immediate response: count to ten or repeat a mantra to soothe ourselves. If we manage to do this, our reaction will be less severe and harmful. Moreover, delaying an impulsive reaction can broadcast strength.

When parents bring up the problematic subject later, they show that they remember and that they have not overlooked their role as parents. Sometimes, when the parent brings up what happened a few hours or days before, the child doesn't remember anymore or, at least, says that. But the parent remembers. This comes as a surprise to the child. Some children even protest when their parents remember,"Why do you keep reminding me about that? It was a long time ago!"

The parent might answer: "Of course, I remember, I think about you all the time!" When parents delay their reaction and return to the topic later, they provide a good example to their children in a number of ways:

- *The parent demonstrates self-control, prevents escalation, and creates conditions for the child to also develop self-control.* Self-control is just as contagious as impulsiveness. It is hard to shout, threaten, and throw a fit when the other person does not react similarly. When parents say quietly, "I do not accept your behavior, but I will consider my reaction," they take the steam out of any mutual incitement. As we know, it takes two to tango. It is less known that it also takes two to have a fit! If the other side is not frightened and does not attack, the rage fades. Therefore the child begins to develop self-soothing skills.
- *Parents show their children they think about them constantly.* It is a significant contribution to children to understand that their parents think about them even in the in-between times, between the moment of confrontation and the moment the parents bring up the problem subject again. There is a special significance to moments when a parents says to a child: "Remember when we took a walk along the lake?" "Remember when I bought you this coat?" "Remember when you got chocolate all over Daddy?" The emotional satisfaction from these situations comes from the child enjoying the contents of the memories, the experience of remembering together, and the very fact that their parent remembers them. Even when parents remind their children of a problem behavior, they are still showing that they remember them and this gives them a sense of continuity. The child's life stops being a collection of disconnected fragments and becomes a more constant sequence. Many theorists have noted the importance of creating a consistent and continuous self-image instead of a disjointed and disorganized view. Children who grow up without the experience of a connecting and unifying thread experience themselves and their world chaotically. When parents develop stability, show self-control, and re-address a difficult subject after a delay, they help to create the sense of continuity critical for child development.

- *The parent contributes to the child by "lending" their memory and thereby helping the child to gradually expand his or her own memory.* This process is like learning to ride a bicycle, with the parent running after the child and stabilizing the bicycle and then letting go, first for a split second, then for a full second, and then for a few seconds. Thus, the child learns to stabilize themselves as a continuation of the parent's stabilization. Similarly, parents can help their child talk about what happened a minute ago, five minutes ago, half an hour ago, the day before. Gradually the child learns how to do it themselves.

Bo, 9, suffered from ADHD. It was hard for him not only to complete a task but also to go back to the same task later because he forgot what steps he had already taken and what he needed to keep doing. When his parents wanted to apply the principle o striking while the iron is cold, it looked like Bo couldn't remember the event his parents were talking about. At first, his parents thought he was faking, but they gradually came to believe he couldn't focus on the relevant incident, partly because he was confusing it with other things that had happened since.

The parents decided to adapt the principle to Bo's particular difficulties. First, they would go back to the subject five minutes after it happened. Then ten minutes. Within a month they worked their way up to having a meaningful conversation with Bo about something that had happened three hours earlier. To help him, they reminded him of the details: "You jumped on the couch, I went over to you, I touched your hand and I asked you to stop. Do you remember what you did then?"

Gradually, Bo started joining the conversation and even enjoyed filling in the missing details. His ability to remember and connect different events took another step forward when his parents made an album of memories and events that had happened in Tom's life. Those stories refered mostly to positive events, but a few problematic incidents were also included. When his grandparents came over, Bo enjoyed looking at the album with them. About a year later Bo enjoyed going back even to old problem events, partly be-

cause they showed him the distance between his present ability and his inability a year earlier.

The Principle of Mellowing: "You don't need to win, just to persist!"

One of the harmful causes of escalation related to punishment is the belief that problems can be solved in one fell swoop. This belief leads to the conclusion that if the problem has not been solved, the punishment was not powerful enough. This turns the relationship between parent and child into a series of "showdowns," which not only fail to achieve their goal but also guarantee that the next battle will be worse than the last one.

The principle of mellowing is based on the opposite assumption about solving complex problems. This is the belief that improvements appear gradually, especially when the parents are persistent. Persistence in this case is not a rigid repetition of the same actions or statements but rather the willingness to continue seeking solutions, patiently striving for even partial improvements, and developing sensitivity to the least signs of positive change.

Liam cut off his relations with his mother, Sinead, following his parents' divorce when he was 13. The rift was very painful because Liam disengaged from his mother's entire family, with whom he had had a warm and close relationship.

About a year after the rift, Sinead, who was grieving bitterly, decided to go for broke in an attempt to break through the barrier of rejection. She arrived unexpectedly at a session between Liam and his psychologist. Liam reacted with an angry outburst, swore at his mother, and fled the room. It took the therapist a tremendous effort to repair the therapeutic relationship.

The mother's attempt to solve the problem "in one go" proved to be a bitter mistake. A few months later, Sinead felt it was time to try again. This time she coordinated her plan with Liam's father, Peter, who felt the continued boycott was damaging to everyone. The therapist, having learned her lesson from the last time, designed a gradual and multilateral plan with both parents. She said, "We must act patiently and aim for a gradual and maybe partial thaw. Any attempt at a total solution might come back to bite us!"

The first step was aimed at increasing Sinead's involvement in Liam's schoolwork. She started to come with Peter to meetings with his homeroom teacher. Liam was informed and did not protest against the change. Sinead started writing a weekly letter to Liam but without trying to convince him to lift the boycott. One copy of her letters was kept by the therapist, on the assumption that Liam might not read them after receiving them. In her letters. Sinead focused on good memories and updates about Liam's grandparents, aunts, and Buffy, his aunt's dog, whom Liam loved. Only once did Sinead reference the rupture in the relationship: she apologized for her surprise appearance at the therapist's. She admitted she had put him on the spot but explained that she was driven by her pain.

Gradually, the therapist started talking to Liam about the possibility of renewing ties with his mother's family. Liam didn't shut the door on that possibility, but he didn't show enthusiasm, either. A few weeks later, his grandmother sent him a letter and birthday present. Peter handed him the letter, but when Liam refused to read it, he did not try to persuade him. Instead, he put the letter on his desk. A few days later, the letter disappeared from the desk. Peter checked, and the letter was not in Liam's garbage can. A month later Liam told his therapist he had received a letter and present from his grandmother.

The signs of change appeared slowly, but the two parents and therapist were paying close enough attention to notice them. Sinead's letters to Liam took on a new format: they were written in an album where other family members added messages, pictures and memories. The therapist let Liam sit with her for a long time with the album after the end of their session. Liam's uncle and grandfather on his father's side asked Liam if he would be willing to meet his maternal aunt. Liam said when he was ready he would say so. Two weeks later a pleasant surprise awaited him: when he came home from school, Buffy was waiting for him in the kitchen. He asked his father who had brought the dog over. Peter said he did, but that his nieces were going to come pick her up. Liam was very excited and did not stop playing with Buffy until the two girls came. When they arrived, he talked to them naturally, as if nothing had happened.

At this point, expanding the relationship with the family was only a question of time. The boycott was no longer a rigid unit but had air vents, and the currents of familial love started seeping in from all sides.

Parents' persistence and the willingness to notice even the smallest sign of change are a special source of strength. As opposed to the authoritarian position, which demands instant obedience, the principle of mellowing draws its power from time itself. A parent who acts on the principle of mellowing opens themselves to changes that may come in unexpected ways in their own time. Such changes are very different from subdued obedience. They allow for beginnings of cooperation and create conditions to internalize values.

Self-control and parental space

In order to develop self-control, parents must be able to calm down, recover, and prepare for what lies ahead. They need protection and breaks. Parents who are continually exposed to aggressive acts and entitled demands are at increased risk of burnout and loss of control. Therefore, it is vital for parents to learn how to defend their bodies, time, privacy, relationships, work and rest.

The first task for parents who wish to deal with problem behaviors in their families is to agree with each other on their red lines. To do so effectively, they must distinguish between actions they will absolutely resist (red lines) and behaviors that, although problematic, can be addressed in a more flexible and tolerant way.

3-Basket Exercise

Uri Weinblatt[5] one of the pioneers of our approach, developed the "three baskets" exercise to help parents decide together on their priorities. Parents are asked to define three imaginary baskets: a red one, a yellow one and a green one.

---

5 Weinblatt, U. (2004), The technique of the three baskets, in H. Omer and A. Schlippe (2004). *Authority and Relationship* (in German), Goettingen, Vandenhoeck & Ruprecht.

The red basket includes absolutely unacceptable behaviors, against which the parents will mount determined resistance.

The yellow basket includes problematic behaviors which the parents are asked to address using softer measures like dialogue, explanations and encouragement.

The green basket includes behaviors the parents may not particularly like, but are willing at least for the moment to overlook in order to focus their efforts on the truly problematic areas.

The goal of the 3-basket exercise is twofold: to lead the parents to talk to each other and reach agreement, and to create a hierarchy that will allow them to focus their efforts instead of spreading them on countless targets. Typical contents that will appear in the red basket are, for example: "violence toward the parents or other members of the family," or "blatant intrusion into the parents' bedroom, bed or study." There are many differences between families when it comes to prioritizing the goals, but protection of the parents and other household members must by no means be put into the yellow basket.

One of the problematic ways parents respond to the three basket exercise is to fill the red basket with a long list of forbidden behaviors. When they are told that this makes their mission impossible, they counter that they cannot give up on any of the subjects. Such parents might say, "What, are we supposed to let her go to bed without brushing her teeth?" Or, "should we put up with him not doing his homework?"

We must understand that the red basket does not encompass the totality of parental action but creates a hierarchy that determines over which (few) points the parents are going to wage a resolute resistance compared with the other goals, which should be pursued using softer means. When parents define a small number of behaviors (two or three) as belonging in the red basket, they can throw all their weight behind acting to prevent them. Parents who establish their status by insisting on a few vital red lines increase their influence in other matters as well. In contrast, parents who jump from one prohibition to another erode their status and find out that each "no" they utter is like a bubble that pops as soon it is released.

The connection between personal space that allows parents to breathe and the ability to do something for their child is illustrated by the instructions given on airplanes for the use of oxygen masks in an emergency. The guidelines are for parents traveling with small children to put on their own masks first and only then put them on the child. The reason is obvious: If a parent tries to put a mask on a child while themselves not breathing, the result might be that both of them won't be able to breathe. In daily life as well, parents must first "put on their own oxygen mask" so that they can develop self-control and do their job effectively.

Johnny (13) was an extreme worrier. He experienced intense anxiety every time he or his parents had even the smallest pain, before every school exam, and at the slightest hint one of his parents was angry at him. He also worried deeply about the risks of war, epidemics, and earthquakes.

His father, Robbie, served as his main comforter. Even though Robbie was a very busy man, he always answered his son's phone calls, but recently these calls increased. Johnny was no longer satisfied by the initial reassurance but would call a second, third, and fourth time to remove all doubts that the risk threatened him. Robbie started getting angry at his son and shouted at him a few times. After these outbursts, he would try to repair the damage and have long conversations with Johnny that sometimes lasted until late at night.

Johnny used to be in therapy, but when he realized his treatment required him to confront his stressful situations actively, he refused to return. He also refused medication because he read that drugs could be addictive.

Robbie heard about a therapeutic program for parents of children with anxiety disorders who refuse to go to therapy themselves.

The grandparents were brought into the picture and agreed to help try to stop the vicious cycle of endless worries and reassuring conversations. The father, the mother, and the two grandparents told Johnny that starting the following day his father would no longer be available to take calls at work. Instead, he could call his grandfather up to three times a day.

Robbie planned a work day outside of his office and "forgot" his cell phone at home. When he got home that night, Johnny met him in bitter tears. Robbie told him, "I'm proud of you!"

Johnny asked him, "What's there to be proud of? I almost died!"

Robbie responded, "That's exactly why I'm proud of you. You survived!"

The next day the routine repeated itself, and when Robbie came home he found his son sitting and playing on the computer. Robbie felt he had learned an important way for helping his son cope with anxiety.

"Mistakes are inevitable but they can be corrected!"

Loss of control is the result of feeling stress. Parents feel they are pushed into the corner, that they lack a degree of freedom and wiggle room, and therefore they respond aggressively. The feelings of stress and urgency can be significantly relieved when parents understand that even if they erred they can always correct their mistakes. The possibility of correcting themselves gives parents an experience of expanding their space for action. Their sense of time changes, and they feel increasingly less trapped in the moment.

Dan, 15, suffered from panic attacks, characterized by shortness of breath, tachycardia, and tremors. Every time he felt there was a chance he might get an attack, he called one of his parents to come pick him up from school.

In consultation with a therapist, the parents, David and Martha, decided to stop picking Dan up from school. When Dan called, they would remind him he must stay at school but could go to the advisor and wait on the chair near the door until he calmed down. The advisor and teacher were part of the plan so that Dan had free access to the advisor's room even when she wasn't there. Two days after the parents' announcement, Dan called his mother and said he was on the brink of panic. Martha repeated in her head that she must control her protective reaction and told him, "Dan, even if it's hard, you'll get through it. If you must, go to the advisor's room and call me again from there in 15 minutes. 'Bye."

Dan immediately called his father,"D..d...dad...I...I I don't know what's happening to me! "I can't breathe... I think... I think it's serious.... I'm choking... I..."

"Dan, I'm on my way!"

Only on the way home did David remember the agreement and the advisor's room. Dan's distress call made him lose control and led him to feel he must immediately go to his son's rescue. On the way home from school, he said to his son," Just don't tell Mom, she won't forgive us for this...'"

The father's initial mistake is understandable. Not responding to such a high level of distress is very difficult without special preparation, but the decision to hide the event from Martha while conspiring with Dan was a serious mistake. The coalition David created with Dan on the way home by saying "don't tell Mom" was likely to weaken the alliance the two parents were trying to build.

At this stage it could still be corrected. In our program for children with anxiety disorders,[6] we offer parents in similar situations a simple act of correction. Both parents enter the child's room and say, "We made a mistake today and gave you the message we did not believe in your ability to deal with your anxiety. We thought about it and understood how wrong that was. We are going to act differently in the future. We will remind you what you need to do, and we will not give in to your anxiety."

Of course, it is important for the parent who was responsible for the mistake to be the one who says this. In this way, the parents convey cooperation instead of deepening the gulf between them. The mishap can be turned into a reminder of parental commitment. In addition, the parents are showing by personal example that mistakes and failures do not mean the end of the effort.

And what about the child's capacity for self-control?

Can children who suffer from a serious disorder, such as severe ADHD, a mental illness, or mental deficiency learn to control themselves?

6 See Lebowitz, E. R. & Omer, H. (2013). *Treating child and adolescent anxiety: A guide for caregivers*. Wiley & Sons

Are these conditions not an absolute obstacle to improvement, due to a deep-rooted mental condition or physiological impairment?

Self-control is not an on-off switch but occurs at different levels, depending on situation, time, skill, and motivation. Following is an example of a conversation with parents of a child suffering from raging outbursts:

Father: I don't think he can control himself. He's been screaming and raging since he was a baby!

Therapist: No doubt he has a low frustration threshold and sometimes even the smallest provocation can set him off. Are there any situations in which he controls himself a little better?

Mother: Yes, when friends come over, he doesn't have outbursts.

Therapist: How does he do it?

Father: They seem to distract him from the things that usually aggravate him.

Therapist: So, he can be distracted. That is one of the important foundations of self-control. How do you think he manages to distract himself?

Mother: I don't think he does. When friends come over, it just happens.

Therapist: Is it possible that nothing aggravates him when his friends come over?

Mother: No, of course he gets aggravated. He hates to lose games. Every time he loses against one of his siblings, he throws a fit. But with his friends, he doesn't have fits.

Therapist: So, he has the ability to distinguish between situations and react accordingly. That is another important element of self-control. Are there other situations in which he has fewer outbursts?

Father: Only when he's with his uncle Moshe, who takes him fishing. There he behaves completely differently.

Therapist: Does he like to fish?

Father: He loves to!

Therapist: Fishing requires a lot of self-control. He seems to have more skills then we thought.

Father: But with his uncle, he doesn't have any frustration; fishing is a whole day of fun. No homework, no need to brush your teeth or take a shower, no schedule. If I could do it, I wouldn't lose my self-control, either.

Therapist: Fishing is a hobby full of frustration. There are hours without any bites, when nothing happens. It's frustrating when a fish gets away. It's even frustrating when another fisherman catches more than we do.

Mother: That's right. His uncle told us that at the beginning he used to be very frustrated that his uncle caught more than he did! But he learned that that's the way it is. It also helped when he started catching more even though he still catches a lot less than his uncle.

Therapist: So, we see that at certain times, in certain situations, and when he has motivation, he can develop the ability to restrain and control himself. The question is how to make that happen in everyday life.

The essential questions parents can ask themselves about their child's capacity for self-control are the following:

- In what situations does the child show more restraint?
- In what situations is he or she the most impulsive?
- What are the best and most problematic times?
- In whose company does he or she function better?
- Did the child ever surprise you by sustaining a difficult situation without having an outburst?
- Did the child ever improve his or her behavior for a while following an unusual event (such as the involvement of the school principal or an unpleasant brush with the law)?

- Does the child behave differently with different teachers?
- Does the child burst out less in front of his father than in front of his mother, or vice-versa?

Parents can also ask themselves if they think in certain situations their child "gives himself or herself license" to let go of their self-control, for instance, when they feel they need to prove they are stronger or when their parents break a rule that they consider sacred. Sometimes, children even tell their parents they are about to show them how out-of-control they are. By doing so, the child shows the ability to actually control his or her own lack of control.

Yuri, 8, was a moody boy. Once after a fight with a friend, he stormed into the house and slammed the door. His mother said: "You don't need to be that angry!"

Yuri replied: "But I want to be angry!"

When they recalled that incident in a pleasant family moment, his parents gave him the nickname "Fury." Yuri smiled proudly.

These questions and considerations change the perception of the child as doomed to uncontrollable outbursts. Instead, we see a picture of a child whose self-control is incomplete but improvable under certain conditions. Even a child with a particularly serious psychiatric diagnosis can improve self-control.

Let's do a simple thought experiment. Let's imagine two boys diagnosed with schizophrenia, undoubtedly one of the most serious diagnoses possible. Let's say they have similar symptoms, and they both respond only partially to medication. The parents of one of them think that because of his illness their son cannot meet demands or maintain a normal routine. The parents of the other one assume that despite his sickness their son can develop his abilities and improve his functioning. The parents of the first boy absorb all of his whims and reactions because they don't believe he has the ability to control himself. The parents of the other boy support any signs of proper functioning, defend themselves and protect the house against his outbursts, and work toward maintaining a normal life and routine.

Now, let's imagine we go back to both families a few years after the illness appeared. We will find an enormous difference between them. In the first family, the child and family will probably be in extremely bad shape. In the second family, despite the difficulties, the family atmosphere will be safe, and there will be areas of normal functioning and significant achievements.

The future outlook for both boys is very different. The first one is facing a life of marginality, very low functioning, and probably living in an institution. The second one will be able to maintain a routine, work, and social relationships. In many cases he will also be able to express his unique skills. He can do all of this despite the symptoms of the disease. His capacity for self-control was not a given. It developed gradually, due to the support, boundaries, and environmental conditions that were established for him.

Conclusion

The development of self-control in parents has been found to be the most important way to change children's problematic behaviors as well as improving parent's influence and authority. Parents are surprised to discover that self-control is actually power. The first principle in the development of self-control is the understanding that parents cannot control their child, only themselves. When they learn to let go of domineering messages such as "you will do what I say!" and replace them with messages such as "we are going to do what we say!" they strengthen themselves. Now they are not dependent on the child's reaction, only on themselves. But they will quickly discover that now the chances of the child cooperating grow considerably.

The second principle for developing self-control is: "Strike while the iron is cold!" This principle releases parents from the urge to respond instantly and provides them with time to plan and prepare. This also shows the child that they remember, which gives their parenting depth. The fact that the child discovers his parents think about and remember him even in between incidents gives the child an experience of continuity.

The third principle in the development of self-control is: "You don't have to win, just to persist!" This principle releases parents from expectations of "all or nothing." Parents gather positive power from persisting and accepting partial improvements as the first signs of bigger changes.

The fourth principle is: "Mistakes are inevitable, but they can be corrected!" This principle adds another layer to self-control by allowing parents to continue improving even after they stumble. By doing so, they provide a personal example that allows the child to admit their own mistakes and make amends for them.

Review and Application

- Restraint and self-control provide strength and status!
- Avoid messages such as "You will do as I say!" Instead, learn to say. "we will do as we say!" Or "it is our duty! We will not give up on you!"
- Learn to delay your responses. When you go back to the problematic issue hours or days later, you are showing your child that you remember, that you don't give up, and that you are still there.
- The expectation for problems to be solved in one fell swoop is one of the biggest traps for parents.
- Learn to see and appreciate small improvements.
- Parents who receive support can control themselves much better!
- Mistakes and misses do not spell the end of developing self-control. On the contrary, they open the possibility of self-correction. Someone who corrects a mistake does not lose status but rather the contrary.
- Self-control is contagious: when you learn how to control yourself, you promote your child's ability to control himself or herself.

Chapter Three

Support and Belonging

"It takes a whole village to raise a child", says a traditional African proverb. However, parents today are much more isolated than they used to be. A high divorce rate, the weakening of the extended family, migration, and seclusion in private houses in anonymous cities all erode the interpersonal fabric which once provided parents with support and legitimacy. Child-rearing has increasingly turned into a task that takes place within the narrow confines of the nuclear family, with the parents and often a single parent carrying the burden alone. Unfortunately, isolated parents are unstable anchors. It only takes a few waves pushing them this way and that to dislodge them.

In this chapter we will discuss the obstacles that deter parents from seeking and receiving support from others. Our goal is to help parents understand that their natural environment contains potential supporters who can help them and their children overcome the difficulties they are experiencing. When parents dare to take action to extract themselves from the isolated bubble in which they are trapped, they rapidly discover they have family members, friends and other allies who are willing to help. It turns out that help is waiting right around the corner. Many things that previously looked stuck and unsolvable suddenly receive new and surprising openings. Also, the supporters help children to go back to feeling like they belong. This is probably the most beneficial outcome of the supporters' entrance into the picture.

The Privacy Reflex: "Why turn to others? I should solve my problems by myself!"

Countless parents react to our proposal to recruit support by saying, "Why turn to others? I should solve my problems by myself!" They feel that recruiting support runs counter to their norms and preferences. In their vision of ideal parenthood, everything essential occurs within the close relationship and direct contact between the parent and child. Common wisdom is that if the personal and intimate relationship is good, all problems will be solved. On the other hand, if there is a problem in the relationship, nothing will help.

This position can be described as "the religion of intimacy." According to this belief, an intimate relationship is not only the supreme value but also the ultimate reason and source of the child's good or bad development. This assumption has become an axiom of an entire generation of parents and psychologists. There's a problem with the child? Something is wrong with the emotional relationship between child and parent. And how do you solve the problem? You have to fix that relationship. Sometimes the assumption is even more narrowly defined: it is the relationship between the mother and the child which is at the center, relegating all other relationships to a marginal role. Even fathers are secondary in this outlook.

This view, however, is fundamentally false. Mothers do not operate in a vacuum. A mother who does not feel surrounded by a supportive network will find it difficult to provide her child with stable support. Alternatively, she will seek in her child all of the support she lacks, thereby building an isolated and closed system, which will impede the child's development. The early involvement of fathers has been proven to be a significant source of resilience.

In certain situations, siblings also play a critical role. Thus, for young children who were left without parents during the Holocaust, the proximity of a sibling often satisfied the developmental deficiency so that these children were able to grow well despite the severe losses they suffered. And as we have already noted, the involvement of grandparents and aunts and uncles can immunize youngsters from delinquency and other at-risk behaviors.

I grew up in São Paulo (Brazil) to a pair of Holocaust survivors. The atmosphere at home was grim. My mother was depressed, and the relationship between my father and mother was problematic. The situation got worse when the entire relationship with my uncle's family was cut off when I was little because of a family dispute. In the absence of grandparents (who perished in the Holocaust), the family isolation was particularly deep.

São Paulo was by then a huge city and my uncle's family lived at the other end of town; two hours travel away on two buses. But I had a fierce need to experience family relations beyond my nuclear family. When I was only 11, I learned how to make the long trip independently. I started spending time at the home of my uncle and aunt, Jechiel and Marta, and went there every Friday night. I went on vacations with them with my three cousins. Eventually I wasn't the only one who gained a lot from that relationship; so did the entire family because I served as a bridge to renew the severed relationship. I believe I received the model for sound family relationships from my uncle's family. I believe that if it weren't for that experience with my uncle's family, I could not have established a good family for my children.

Parents are often in a delicate situation vis-à-vis their children for several reasons:

- children know their parents' weaknesses and red buttons;
- children often take their parents for granted so that their services or demands become meaningless;
- parents are exceedingly sensitive to children's distress signals and tend to rush to their rescue even when they can cope by themselves.
- In addition to all of this, there is a unique parental difficulty because many children, especially in adolescence, feel the need to assert their self-determination in a way that conflicts with their parents. When this is the case, parents' attempts at influence often lead to the opposite of the desired reaction.

Here are some questions parents can ask in order to assess whether these situations occur to them:

- Does my child know how to provoke me so that I can't help myself?
- Does my child know how to pressure me so that I succumb to demands?
- Does our child take advantage of the gaps between us parents?
- Does my child take everything we give for granted?
- Does my child often make us rush to his or her aid by crying or other distress signals?
- Do I feel that my words fall on deaf ears?
- Does my child ignore me?
- Do I feel that my child is dependent and babyish when I am around?

These are all aspects in which the special intimacy between parent and child can lead to problematic outcomes. The desirable solution is not increasing the distance, which may be unbearably difficult both for the parent and the child, but increasing the support network, so that other people can enter the picture in places where the parent-child relationship is so intense that it is hard for the parent to breathe and for the child to grow. Parenthood that is sealed within the parent-child bubble is often more painful and less effective. It is more painful because any attempt to loosen the knot and open up a functional space for both parties may be experienced as an unbearable rift. It is less effective because the intimacy and dependency work against the natural process of maturation.

The Shame Factor: "Exposure will lead to unbearable shame!"

The shame factor deters parents in two ways: they find it difficult to overcome the exposure barrier, which can place them in an unfavorable light in the eyes of others, and they are even more afraid that the experience of shame will be traumatic for their child. For parents to better cope with the subject of shame, they must understand an important point about the critical role of the emotion of shame in child development.

The experience of shame is always unpleasant but not always harmful. On the contrary, it plays a critical role in developing the child's sense of belonging and moral development. The difference between a harmful and constructive experience of shame has to do with the broader interpersonal and emotional context in which the shame is experienced. Experiences of shame that come with messages of rejection and ostracism are not only severely unpleasant but also potentially damaging. Shaming punishments that include marginalization, humiliation. or derogatory expressions carry a sharp message of lack of belonging. Although the expectation is for the child to renew belonging after the expression of regret, in many cases this simply does not happen. Some children refuse to sustain the humiliating process and prefer to suffer as much as needed as long as they will not have to bow their heads. Others, forced into submission, may nurture resentment in a way that undermines both their sense of belonging and their loyalty to the values their caretakers wish to impart to them. It is very different when the child experiences shame but in a context that conveys support and belonging.

In our program for coping with children's violence, we make special use of "public opinion," but the "public" in question comprises a group that has a positive attitude toward the child. To do this, we help parents or teachers create a group of supporters composed of members of the extended family, friends, school faculty, and sometimes other meaningful figures (such as a sports coach or youth counselor). When the child commits a violent act (such as hitting his sister), the members of the group receive a detailed report. Then, one or two members of the group contact the child and say: "I know you hit your sister yesterday. You know I care about you. I think highly of you, and I am sure you can get this under control! I am also willing to help you avoid getting into such situations because hitting your sister is violence and must stop." This message includes three positive components: a message of love and connection, a message of trust and appreciation, and a message of willingness to help. This creates a positive context, which helps the child contain the experience of shame. The combination of messages of appreciation, belonging, and support, along with an honest and direct reference to the problem behavior, strengthens the child's ability to tolerate the shame. Such experiences are critical for proper development.

The understanding that shame is not only a tolerable but even vital experience helps many parents overcome the barrier of exposure and ask for help. For some parents, though, this is not enough to overcome their own shame barrier. They feel that exposing their difficulties will show them to be failed parents. These parents can overcome the shame barrier by learning to ask for help in a way that raises their self-esteem rather than lowering it. For instance, the parent can tell their friends or relatives: "You can imagine it has not been easy for me to take this step and share our difficulties with our daughter. But our concern for her condition and her future led me to dare to turn to you!" Parents who reveal their problem in this way shows themselves to have conquered their own feelings of shame for the sake of their daughter and family. That is an act of courage, not weakness.

Another kind of message emphasizes the special value of the supporter in the eyes of the seeker. For instance: "You know I don't like to talk about problems and sometimes it's hard for me to ask for help. But I thought that if I hid my problems from you, I would be ignoring the special place you have in our and our children's lives!" In this statement. the request is leveraged by the respect and trust given to the supporter.

These statements contain a deep secret of helping acts: they impart value both to the giver and to the asker. In the supporters' meetings we hold there is an atmosphere of benefit for all: the parents receive support, and the supporters gain from the privilege of helping the child and family.

The Fear of Looking Weak

The instant reaction of many parents and teachers when asked to recruit support is: "Then the child will think I'm weak!"

Parents can fortify themselves against the fear of being seen as weak if they understand that the power reflected by a raised hand, an intimidating shout, or a deterring punishment is less important and less "strong" then the power revealed by broad shoulders. A power that says "we!" is more valid and legitimate than a power that says "me!" For parents who understand this it will not be hard to respond to the child's defiance when they activate supporters. They will say to the child: "Of course, I'm going to your grandparents and aunts and uncles. We have all decided we will not tolerate violence anymore!" Or, "when you disappear from home, we all mobilize! We will never give up on you!"

Such statements turn the defiance upside down. Instead of shrinking in shame for being exposed as weak, the parent can feel proud as the representative or leader of a group committed to defending against violence, destruction and self-risk. Parents who act in this way free themselves from the duel mentality which may have previously characterized their relationship with the child. There is nothing more effective against the child's defiance than the position: "What, didn't you know? We're all together against violence!"

Elizabeth is a single mother who was completely exhausted from her power struggles with her 11-year-old son, Lee. She felt that the more she threatened and demanded, the more stubborn and resistant he became. Sometimes, she felt he enjoyed arguing with her for argument's sake. She could see no way out of the labyrinth. She had already been to see several advisors and tried the kind way and the hard way. Lee was resistant to persuasion, reinforcement, and seduction, as well as to threats and punishments. One of his favorite sayings was, "What's the worst thing you can do to me?" As if he were inviting her to look in her toolbox for another punishment, only so he could trip her up again.

In conversations with the therapist in our clinic two objectives were set: (1) to learn to get out of any duel and power struggle, and (2) to build a support system that would enable the mother to speak and act as "we." To emphasize the retreat from any power struggle, Elizabeth composed with her supporters (the child's grandparents, her two siblings, and her adult daughter) a certificate that attested that Lee was "an invincible child.; he cannot be defeated because he is the kind of boy who would rather die than surrender." The certificate was signed by all of the supporters as well as the dog, probably Lee's most beloved creature.

The certificate was printed on parchment and hung in Lee's room. Two days after the certificate was given, Lee purposely broke one of his mother's vases. That night, a few hours later, Elizabeth entered his room with his aunt and uncle. They sat down and told him they would stay there and wait for an idea of how he was go-

ing to compensate his mother for the damage. Lee pointed at the certificate and said, "You don't have a chance. You said yourself I am invincible!"

His uncle answered, "That's right, you are invincible! But we all have the duty to resist violence even if we do not win!"

The room fell silent for a long moment. Lee offered no compensation because it would have injured his pride. Two days later, his grandparents came to him and said, "We can't make you compensate your mother if you don't want to, but we can collect a compensation from you simply because justice demands it. We decided to take back our promise to buy you a new PlayStation for Christmas. Instead, the money will go to replacing the vase you broke."

Lee was given the chance to reconsider the option of compensating his mother, but he maintained his resistance. When on Christmas he did not receive the gift, he pretended he didn't care.

In the past, the mother may have gotten into a futile discussion with him about how he was only harming himself. This time she avoided all comment. Instead, the new vase was placed in the place of the old one without saying a word. The mother reported to the therapist, "I never imagined I would feel so good because of receiving support. I don't feel the need to shout anymore! Instead, I can speak quietly because I am part of a choir!"

Even though at no moment did Lee bend his head or express regret, his behavior changed. He no longer had a partner for arguments.

Fear of the Child's Response

For some families, the decision to disclose the child's problems, even to close people like grandparents, can be the shattering of a sacred taboo. The parents are afraid that exposure will lead the child to severe outbursts and maybe a serious mental crisis. In some cases, the child frankly threatens that if the parent tells things about them, they will react extremely.

Following are some questions parents can use to hold a productive self-scrutiny or dialogue about their fear of the child's reaction.

Do I think that my child will feel they are alone against everyone?

This fear is related to the image of the supporters as "ganging up" on the child. Actually, involving the supporters is done in exactly the opposite way. Following a problematic event, only one or two close people approach the child. The approach is always done in a positive spirit as we clarified when we talked about the experience of constructive shame. Under these conditions, there are good chances the child's positive tendencies will come to the fore.

Deep in their hearts, the vast majority of children want to improve their problematic behavior pattern but don't know how. Even children who seem determined to maintain their raging and violent patterns wish their problem were solved and that they were not induced to further outbursts.

This is true even for delinquent youth or substance abusers. Deep inside they have positive voices and secret wishes to improve, but the positive voices have a hard time being effective. As soon as the child discovers people are willing to make an effort for them, and especially when instead of rebuking and demanding they address them with respect, the positive voices get louder.

Will my child not be terribly mad at me?

Indeed, parents' appeal for help sometimes draws a reaction of rage. Some children do accuse their parents of betrayal and violating their privacy.

There are also children who explicitly forbid their parents from talking about them with strangers. These children know well that privacy is a sacred value in our society, and its mere mention brings their parents to stand at attention and drop their intention of exposing the problem. Parents should be aware of this and instead of falling into the trap answer patiently, "These problems are not only your problems; they are also our problems!" This expresses the parents' basic right to seek and receive help.

Parents' ability to tolerate the child's anger at them for supposedly violating the child's privacy increases when they understand they are protecting the entire household. When parents understand this, they also convey it to the child well. The message "we decided to ask for help because we are all suffering from this!" is highly legitimate. When talking to the child, the grandfather, aunt or friend can say simply: "But of course! It is the whole family's problem!"

The child's rage will dissipate for another reason as well: the exposure is a unique event after which the wheel cannot be turned back. Once the situation is exposed, the only choice is to get used to the new situation. Support, on the other hand, is an ongoing process. The benign presence of the supporter will exist today, tomorrow and the next day. The impact of the support process gradually outweighs the impact of the exposure. All it takes is for the child to have one experience of receiving real help to understand that exposing the secret works in their favor.

What if the child has a mental breakdown after learning a secret was exposed?

This is one of the horror scenarios parents carry in their heads. Sometimes, there is even fear that children will harm themselves whether they have hinted about that before or not. Some parents feel their child's mental stability is a very fragile thing and all it takes is the slightest breeze to topple it over. Our research indicates the opposite is true. Involving supporters is one of the best guarantees to improving the child's mental state, whereas the conditions of isolation and secrecy in which the problems are kept are among the main causes of their persistence. It is important to note that in many hundreds of cases we treated we have not seen even a single case in which involving supporters led to a mental crisis. To the contrary, we have witnessed numerous cases in which the help of the supporters extracted a child or adolescent from such a crisis.

Of course, it is important to consider carefully what to tell the supporters and how. It is important to consider how to treat intimate information such as sexual events or orientation. The right to privacy in these areas is maintained even when involving supporters. Sometimes, support can be obtained for these subjects as well by distinguishing between the roles of different supporters. For instance, a friend or relative can be found who can gain the child's trust and talk about those areas. However, these are not subjects that should be disclosed to the whole group. Supporters understand when they are told: "There are intimate issues with which our child is struggling, and which she discusses with her uncle whom she trusts."

We would like to note a key rule: harming others or oneself is never a private event. Any such harm is an event that concerns many people. We include in this category events of violence or abuse of siblings or parents as well as self-harm whether by cutting, dangerous diets, or other destructive actions. Nor does the threat of suicide, whether demonstrative or implied, belong to the category of intimate events. To the contrary, threatening suicide is one of the most violent actions that exist. With one act, the child threatens to destroy not only his or her own life but also that of the parents. The fact that the harm is directed inward does not make the threat less violent or more private. When family members are informed they are asked to talk to the child openly. If the child protests the supposed violation of privacy, say simply, "Your life and physical integrity are not private matters; they concern everyone who loves you!"

What should we do if he runs away from home? Or threatens we will never see him again?

The best way to approach horror scenarios is to develop a coping plan. A child who threatens to run away, or who already disappeared in the past, requires tightening parental vigilance and expanding the circle of people the parents can turn to if necessary. The preparation for such situations significantly strengthens parental presence. Parents' ability to seek help and contact people in the child's environment (friends, friends' parents and other figures like the child's teachers, sports coach, shopkeeper or owner of dance club) releases them from the feeling they are trapped in a bubble. To prepare for the threat of running away, parents compile in advance a list of names and phone numbers of the child's friends and other figures. With a little work, any parent can make themselves such a list.

The loneliness barrier: "We have no supporters!"

Many parents respond to the suggestion of creating a support group by saying they have no one who supports them. The experience of loneliness and lack of supporters is typical of many families. The modern family is often a social island. But loneliness is not only an objective situation, it is also a habit and mentality. In our experience, many of the parents who thought they had no potential supporters were surprised to discover the opposite was true when they dared test the limits of their loneliness with a few simple questions:

Are members of the extended family in the picture? Have I asked for their help?

Often the initial answer to this question indicates the supposed barriers. For example, the grandparents live far away. The grandparents are old, sick, or anxious. The parents' relationship with their siblings is not close enough. The uncle is an old-fashioned type of person who, if he knew what was happening, would only be angry and disapproving. The parents' friends are busy with themselves.

These obstacles do not withstand serious scrutiny. This is especially noticeable when it comes to involving grandparents. Living far away is not an insurmountable obstacle because phone and digital communication facilitate significant support despite the distance. Sometimes, there is frequent and even daily contact with the grandparents, but the parents never thought of using that connection for the problematic areas. The failure to involve grandparents increases the emotional distance and voids the relationship of real value. This makes the conversations shallow and insignificant. The grandparents receive a false picture of the family, and in this way the parents actually exclude them from traditional roles that could add meaning to their lives. The same goes for reservations because of their age or tendency to worry. The wish to spare the grandparents trouble and worry does not benefit them. The fact that the parents keep them in their ignorance only causes their ailments to fill their entire consciousness.

Peter (12) tended to keep to himself, often refusing to leave his room for days in a row. His parents, Lara and Eugene, were at first reluctant to involve Peter's grandfather because he suffered from an orthopedic ailment. In the past, Peter had enjoyed watching soccer with his grandfather but that stopped as he increasingly secluded himself during the last year.

Ultimately, the parents decided to tell the grandparents about the change and their concern about Peter. The grandfather started texting Peter during important games, which each saw in their own home. A couple of weeks later Peter visited his grandfather and they watched a game together. Then Peter joined a soccer team. Peter's grandfather started coming to Peter's games in spite of his difficulties. Obviously, both sides profited from the grandfather's support.

Aunts, uncles, cousins, parents' friends often turn out to be valuable sources of support. The acts of being involved and giving help serve to restore family cohesion. Cousins, especially older ones, can play a role similar to older siblings. Sometimes, parents are surprised that the cousins are willing to devote time and attention to their children. But the aunts and uncles are not surprised; they know their children and know that if asked they would respond positively. It is important to understand that the required help does not have to be intensive. Sometimes, it is enough to be willing to invite the cousin once every month or two to spend time together. Often, a cousin will be found who is willing to help in a specific area such as homework or sports coaching. In many cases, aunts and uncles decide to take their nieces and nephews on a vacation. Such events can deeply change the sense of family belonging.

Do I have a good relationship with the homeroom teacher? Or with anyone from the school faculty?

Parents don't usually think about teachers as potential supporters. The common attitude toward teachers today is often critical. When the child has problems at school, relations between parents and teachers might deteriorate to mutual accusations. This not only works against both sides but seriously harms the child. The more disconnected school and home are from each other, the less consistent and coherent the child's life will be. Many parents are surprised to discover that improving relations with the school not only brings relief to problems at school but also elevates their status. This happens because the child learns that their parents are more involved and informed. Parents who manage to maintain a good relationship with the school expand their vision and influence. The parent's authority reverberates the teacher's and is reverberated by it in turn. When the parent knows basic things like details of the school material, homework, events in the classroom and the child's social situation, parental presence in the child's awareness grows. On the other hand, when the child sinks beneath the parental radar because of an absence of coordination with the teachers, parental presence is eroded. When parents and teachers renew their cooperation, the child feels as if both parties are taking care of them together.

Do I know my child's friends and their parents? Am I in touch with at least one of them?

One of the difficult features of modern society is anonymity and seclusion, with each of us living in our own bubble. Often the homes of a child's friends are like an alien world. Parents feel uncomfortable approaching, asking, and talking to the parents of their children's friends as if contacting them would be a violation of unwritten codes. Often, parents feel uncomfortable even to initiate small talk with their children's friends when they visit their home.

Some children choose not to let their parents spend time with their friends: as soon as their friends enter the house, the child smuggles them into their room, where they will be protected against the gaze or random encounter with their parents. As long as parents accept those unwritten prohibitions with resignation, they will remain disconnected from their child's social world and alien to its influences.

Parents usually respond positively to the suggestion of overcoming the rift that separates them from their child's friends and their parents. They understand that knowing the friends and being able to talk to them and their parents is an essential part of their role. The very fact that the child tries to prevent that is a warning sign indicating problematic processes. The ability to talk to the child's friends and their parents is critical for parents for several reasons:

- it enables parents to assess whether the child is keeping problematic company;
- it opens a window into the child's plans and activities;
- it enables coordinating activities, exits and returning times;
- it enables the parents to look for the child if and when they try to evade them;
- it enables coordination between the parents of the two families; and
- it increases the legitimacy of parental decisions, especially ones made in coordination with other parents.

Chloe noticed that Vivi (13) came home smelling like cigarettes and alcohol after being at a party at her classmate's house. Chloe had recently begun to be concerned that Vivi had joined a group of new girlfriends, who she felt were taking her daughter in bad directions.

Chloe took advantage of the parent-teacher night that was planned for that week to contact two other mothers, share her concerns and exchange phone numbers with them. The three mothers decided to cooperate to find out more and, if necessary, intervene to prevent smoking and drinking alcohol at parties. They talked to the parents of the classmate at whose party Vivi had probably smoked and drunk alcohol. The parents said they had come home late that night and found out the children had gone into the parents' liquor cabinet and taken a bottle of whiskey.

The group of parents then decided to talk with their children about the discovery and the coordination between them. They told their children they had all decided to inquire in advance about every party or social activity, to coordinate with the hosting parents and to agree on ways to make sure there were no alcohol or cigarettes at parties. The parents contacted several other parents from the class and told them about their plans.

The requests from the supporters are modest, and each supporter can help as best as he or she can. Gradually it becomes clear that certain supporters play a more central role while others follow the process from the sidelines. However, the very fact that they know and the child knows that they know changes the ecology of the problem. That is because conditions of concealment and secrecy are like a hotbed for many behavioral problems. As soon as the problems are exposed, the situation changes fundamentally.

How can parents create an embracing circle that gives the child a sense of belonging?

One of the main contributions of a support network is giving the child a sense of belonging. The best support teams are the ones that extend to the child an invitation to belong. Of course, this is not a formal invitation but rather an attitude that is communicated in every contact. The parents' and supporters' actions tell the child, "We care about you!" "We are with you!" "You have a place in our heart!" "We think about you all the time!" "You are not alone!"

Even children that ignore these messages demonstratively are not indifferent to them. Gradually the invitation to belong makes an impression. The change is not evident all at once but gradually, first hesitantly, then more and more fully. For the parents, too, it is a critical process because when they realize that recruiting supporters is a positive and inviting step directed toward the child, their reservations decrease. Following are several principles and messages that greatly strengthen the positive aspect of involving supporters.

"We have our own tribe!"

An isolated parent is not a source of attraction for the child's need to belong. As children grow up, they learn to read the social map and assess the quality of relationships as well as the standing of the people surrounding them. They look at their parents' relationship with each other and their immediate environment and draw conclusions about their position and status. Parents who are seen as secluded and isolated lose status in their child's esteem. This changes when parents break out of their seclusion and receive broad support. When the parent and supporters start to talk in the language of "we," the child receives the message, "We have our own tribe!" The child slowly understands that the map has changed. From here on, it is harder for the child to ignore a parent, now that the parent is backed up by supporters. Many parents are surprised to discover that even when their child protests, he or she begins to respect them.

In a study we did in our clinic, we discovered that single parents, precisely the ones who need support the most, are also those who have the most difficulty with the idea of recruiting supporters. Maybe the reason is that these parents are much more used to acting alone. Indeed, the explanation they give is that turning to supporters contradicts their approach as parents. We believe this position misses a simple truth: an isolated parent risks losing their power to activate the child's need to belong. The child may remain dependent on that parent in terms of concrete needs but become increasingly less willing to accept that parent as an authority, a guide, and a source of values. One girl expressed this in especially cruel language. She said, "Everything I did is because I did not want to be lonely like my mother!"

This changes when supporters tell the child, "When your mother turned to us, we understood she deserves all the support possible!" Or "we agree with your parent on this subject!" These messages show that the parent not only dared to break out of the trap of loneliness but was also found to be worthy of support. Children have sensitive instincts for the social map. Therefore, when a parent receives broad support, their standing in the eyes of the child improves.

Reducing control messages paves the way to renewed belonging

It is important to pave an easy way for the child to promote their willingness to belong. Control messages do the exact opposite. When a child receives the authoritarian message, "if you don't obey, then...," they feel a strong urge to respond by disobedience. They will then look to satisfy their need for belonging elsewhere. Messages such as "you will do as I say!" give many adolescents the feeling they have no choice but to resist with all their might. It is very different when the parents, with the help of their supporters, say, "We will do what we say!" Such a message achieves two goals: it strengthens the parental standing and lowers the step the child needs to climb up in order to belong. Now belonging is no longer the opposite of autonomy. Cooperation is no longer equal to surrender.

Andy (15) and his family were caught in a severely negative atmosphere because of his aggression and harassment of his sisters. In one case when he called his older sister an obscene sexual name, his sister's boyfriend rushed to her defense and slapped him on the cheek. Following that event, Andy told his parents that every time his sister's boyfriend came over, he was going to leave the house for a few days. His father, Morris, told him decisively, "It's my home, and I invite anyone I want to it!"

Andy responded by slamming the door behind him and disappearing for two days. Now the father and son were caught in a power struggle, with each party seeing every concession as an unbearable surrender.

Morris's brother, who was brought into the picture, contacted Andy, and told him, "Come over to us for the weekend! The two of us will go on an outing together, and let's look for a respectable way to get you out of the trouble you got into at home!"

Andy answered him, "I do not belong to a family that is willing to invite someone over who hits me!"

His uncle told him, "On the weekend, you will belong to us! We will be happy to hug you!"

Andy felt that his uncle's invitation gave him the message of both respect and belonging. Following the weekend at his uncles' place, Andy got invitations from other relatives. He accepted several invitations even though his relatives told him openly that they were acting in coordination with his parents. Some of his supporters told him point blank, "All of us, and especially your parents, believe that both you and your sisters deserve to live with a feeling of security in your home!"

Andy felt embraced and supported. His parents started to come visit him when he was staying with other relatives. The atmosphere gradually calmed down. Two months later he sat next to his sister's boyfriend at the table at his parents' house. His demeaning behavior toward his sister disappeared.

Adolescents listen better when supporters come into the picture

Many parents, especially of adolescents, experience their children beginning to question their positions, knowledge, and guidance. This should be seen as part of natural development. Whereas little children look to their parents for the answers to every question, adolescents do not want to rely solely on their parents anymore but seek additional sources of knowledge and guidance.

In fact, from a young age, the child benefits from the environment echoing and enriching their parents' attitudes. For instance, when a mother tells a child how she learned certain things from her father or mother, the child feels held within a family community that passes down knowledge and wisdom. A similar process occurs when friends and family members tell the child something special about their father or mother.

Suddenly, the parents stop being the isolated, shallow, and occasionally annoying figures—almost like stick figures—with whom the child clashes every day and are perceived as having more depth.

In my adolescence, I distanced myself from my parents. In all of my preferences and choices I became "anti-," so much so that I was enthralled by certain positions or opinions simply because they were the opposite of my parents' opinions. Following my strong urge for independence, I left Brazil, where we were living at the time, and moved to Israel alone when I was eighteen.

A few months later, my aunt and uncle visited the country, and I spent many hours with them. On that occasion, my uncle told me how my father, my mother, and he ran away from Poland together following the persecution of Jews after World War II when several residents of their town were murdered. The three of them had to travel through five countries until they found refuge in Italy, where they stayed for two years. My uncle told me how my father managed to overcome obstacles along the way, especially at border crossings, with cunning and daring worthy of an adventure film. My uncle's stories were especially important to me because he never exaggerated or embellished.

A few months later my father came to Israel and took me on my first trip to Europe. We spent the most intimate two weeks together we had ever had. During those two weeks, I began to hold my father in new esteem. He took me to the Lido club in Paris, but they didn't let us in because I was not wearing a tie. It was late at night, and there was no place open to buy a tie. My father stepped aside, took off the belt of my raincoat, and tied it around my neck with an especially decorative bow. When we entered the Lido and passed the same doorman who previously prevented us from entering, my father asked him in French: "Isn't that a nice tie?" The doorman smiled in agreement (he surely noticed it was a nonstandard tie). I may not have remembered this event so vividly had it not been for the stories I had heard from my uncle about my father's ability to get himself out of tight spots.

Later on our journey I had more surprises. In Italy, I heard my father speak Italian differently with different people. I asked him why, and he explained: "I was talking Neapolitan to that one, the Barese dialect to that one, and plain Italian to the other ones."

It sounded familiar to me. My uncle told me how in the concentration camp my father had learned the languages and dialects of Lithuanians, Ukrainians, and even a few sentences for communicating with Hungarians, and how he had rehearsed a lot to memorize them so that he could make little deals that were critical to survival.

My uncle's stories enabled me to see my father in a new light. On that joint trip, my father's actions connected with my uncle's stories, creating for me a basis of appreciation toward him, which stayed with me until his death and thereafter.

Adolescents listen better to others than to their parents. When they talk to the child their words will be connected but not identical to those of the parents. This mixture of difference and similarity makes the supporters' voice especially relevant. It does not weaken the parents' voice but creates new nuances and directions that can pique interest and make an impact.

Back to the principle of delayed action: giving the child pause to recover

The principle of delayed action that is embeded in our saying "strike the iron while it is cold!" provides parents with more self-control, prevents escalation and conflagration, and strengthens the parents' position by showing the child and themselves that they remember. Those are not all of the advantages of this principle. Parents who can calmly tell their child, "you don't need to answer now, you may take your time!" provide a pause for the child to reconsider and express the positive voices inside his or her mind. When the parents give the child a pause to recover, they remove the obstacle of rage that is blocking the way to a positive reaction.

On the other hand, when parents make conclusive demands like "You have to admit you lied!" "Clean it up right now!" or "Apologize to your sister!" the child feels obliged to refuse even at the cost of getting punished.

Even when the child is given a pause, they may still need help to take a step in a positive direction. This is where the supporters can play a significant role. When the grandfather or family friend contacts the child the next day, tells the child they have been updated about what happened, and offers to help find a dignified solution, chances are better the child will respond positively. If the child still refuses (for many children, refusal is a matter of honor), the supporter can say, "You don't have to answer me now. Just know that when I say a dignified solution, I mean a solution that will maintain your dignity. I hope you'll just think about it!"

This gives the child additional pause, and the honor barrier is lowered another notch. Also, the supporter's entry into the picture creates new options for belonging: now the child has another opening to belong through the grandfather or friend. It is usually not as hard to go through this opening as through the direct opening offered by the parents. Through the supporter, the child can reenter the family network from the flank and not head on. It is like someone wishing to enter a party without being noticed, but once they are in, they become part of the celebration.

Erwin's (11) favorite expression was "it's not fair!" He felt his parents always discriminated against him compared to his sister Shirley, 9, and he got back at her over this at every opportunity. When his parents scolded or punished him, he shut down and entrenched himself in his resentment. His parents walked on eggshells around him and often even preferred to ignore his picking on his sister.

His aunt Alicia had a special touch with Erwin. He was always glad when she came over and even more so when she took him out even though she always took Shirley and him together. When he was with his aunt, he rarely expressed envy of Shirley.

Erwin's parents sought counseling and made an "announcement"[7] *to Erwin, saying that they had decided to resist his violence and harassment of Shirley and them. Following the announcement, Erwin controlled himself for a few days but then went back to picking on Shirley even more. In the evening, both parents went into Erwin's room and told him he had to compensate Shirley for hurting*

7 The announcement process is described in chapter 5.

her. They said, "We don't expect you to make an offer now. You can think about it in your free time!"

Erwin protested as usual that his parents weren't fair, but they did not get into an argument with him. The next day, Alicia invited him over. Erwin was glad, especially since he was invited without his sister. A little while later, his aunt told him, "As you can imagine, I've been told what happened. You know, I'm very fair with you. What I'm going to offer you is a way for you to be fair with me, too. Why fair with me? Because the two of you are my niece and nephew, and when you hurt Shirley, you hurt me, too. I want us to think together how you can do something nice for Shirley in a way that maintains your dignity and is also fair to me!"

Erwin was struck silent. It was hard for him to continue the conversation.

Alicia told him, "I don't want an answer now. I have an idea that could maintain your dignity very well, but let's talk about it later."

After she had piqued his curiosity, Alicia took Erwin to the kitchen and gave him her famous freshly-baked chocolate chip cookies. They were simply Erwin and Shirley's favorite thing in the whole world. It might look as if Erwin was given a prize for his bad behavior, but the purpose of the intervention was not to use rewards and punishments but rather to facilitate an act of reparation toward Shirley and make an opening for Erwin to improve his sense of belonging to his family. Later, Alicia made her offer. They would go into Shirley's room together. Erwin would give her the cookies he kept especially for her along with a short letter in which he apologized for not being fair to her. Alicia also signed the letter as a witness, which made it much easier for Erwin.

The next day, his father told Erwin he was very impressed by how fair he had been in his reaction. This turned the concept of fairness into a unifying concept instead of a divisive one in the family.

Gestures of reconciliation and connection

Gestures of reconciliation and connection by the parents contribute to reopening the relationship between parent and child that sometimes becomes circumscribed by recurrent conflicts.

The effectiveness of these gestures is multiplied when supporters are involved in the process. This is because supporters validate and increase the significance of parental gestures by their participation in the process.

(1) Haley, (7), repeatedly challenged her parents with her stubborn refusal of every request. Getting ready to leave the house in the morning was torturous. The parents got used to bracing themselves for a rough struggle. On Saturday morning, the parents prayed Haley would wake up a little later so that they could at least enjoy a stolen hour of rest.

To get out of the maze and put some space into the relationship that got narrower and narrower, the parents decided to make Haley a "good girl album." This is a gesture designed to remind parents and child of the good sides of their character and relationship. The parents fill the album with pictures and stories of pleasant events, pictures the child drew, and/or documentation of their nice sides. Members of the extended family are invited to contribute to the album, which is always placed in a central place in the home.

Haley responded enthusiastically to the idea, especially when her grandparents, uncles, and aunts asked to see the album and added from their memories. Working on the album helped not only Haley but also her parents. They saw her less in the narrow light of the confrontations and more as a child greater than the sum of her difficulties.

One day, the mother surprised herself when she told her husband and the grandparents, "Maybe it's not only the good girl album! It's also the good mother album because it shows me that I am more than an angry and scolding mother!"

(2) Johnny, 13, was sitting in front of the computer, playing a loud shooting game when his mother, Martha, knocked on his closed

door. Johnny shouted impatiently, "What do you want? I'm busy!" and continued shooting the enemies on the screen.

Martha answered through the door, "I made your favorite coconut cake. I brought you a piece!"

Johnny did not stop shooting and screamed: "I don't need any favors from you!"

Martha, who had prepared in advance for the possibility of rejection, answered, "I made you the cake because I'm your mother. I'm putting it in the fridge for you!" And she did.

Johnny continued ignoring his mother. To maintain his pride, he did not touch the cake. A week later, Martha repeated the gesture. Johnny's uncle came to visit in the afternoon and said, "Do you mind if I have some of the cake your mother made you? This cake is irresistible!"

Now Johnny's dilemma became bigger: why should others enjoy the cake and not him? Johnny had a slice of cake with his uncle. The next day, his grandparents came over. They told Johnny: "Is there any more of your mother's peace cake? Or did you eat it up?"

Johnny answered, "Not only me; Uncle Moshe did, too!"

His grandparents laughed, and Johnny smiled. His grandfather said, "Your mom already told us the cake was used up! So, now it's your time to show nobility. I'm buying pizza for us all, and you have to ask your mother and brother which toppings they want. We'll go get the pizza together!"

Statements That Increase the Child's Desire to Belong

Over the years we have collected many statements by parents of children who entrenched themselves in tough positions of rejection or boycott of their parents. In many cases, the messages were transmitted by supporters, among other reasons because the children were unwilling to receive the messages directly from their parents. Sometimes, the parents left a piece of paper with the message on the child's desk. Later one of the supporters told the child they had talked about it with the parents. This gives the parents' gestures of connection and belonging a semi-public status. The following examples have become a model for many parents who used similar formulas or developed other versions to express similar messages.

a) Messages of loyalty and devotion:
"I am your father. and I will always be your father!"
"If you're ever in trouble, I will do everything I can to help you!"
"Deep down, I'm sure that if Grandma or I were ever in trouble, you would come to our assistance!"

b) Messages of appreciation and pride:
"I'm proud of your resilience!"
"Even when you fight with us, I'm amazed at your ability to keep it up!"

c) Expressions of belonging:
"I will do everything to show you that you have a home, that you have a safe place, and that you have a family you belong to!"
"In this family, it is 'all for one and one for all!' I'm sure that if one of us were in danger you would show us your worth!"

d) Expressions of faith and hope:
"I believe in you and in your ability to get over it!"
"I've seen you get out of bigger trouble! You may not remember but I do!"

e) Expressions that reduce control messages:
"We would all like you to start talking to your mother again. But nobody can make you!"
"Nobody can force you to feel you belong!"
"You can't be pushed. It might take a long time until you feel you can improve your relationship with us!"

The messages of belonging are a "standing invitation," that allows the child to respond if and when the child is ready. Involving supporters increases breathing room for response, partly because the child can choose to respond through them or with their mediation without feeling they are giving up a position or "matter of principle" in which they are entrenched.

Conclusion

Parental isolation is one of the main causes for losing the ability to withstand currents that threaten to pull the child to undesirable places. Nonetheless, it is still difficult for many parents to turn to supporters because of the privacy reflex, the fear of looking weak, the fear of shame or harm, the fear of the child's response, and the feeling there are no available supporters. In our work with parents, we have demonstrated that parents are able to overcome their hesitation and turn to supporters when their reservations are addressed, e.g., when they understand that sanctifying privacy can undermine belonging. Or when they understand that maintaining a cloak of secrecy is not proof of loyalty but sometimes the exact opposite of loyalty. Or when they understand that the child needs to feel shame in a supportive context when he or she behaves offensively.

Parents quickly discover that seeking help does not make them look weak but the opposite. The broad shoulders they get to share raise their esteem in the eyes of the child and themselves.

Many parents also understand that their isolation is not a decree of fate but may be the result of habit and mistaken assumptions about the nature of seeking help. These understandings are translated into action when parents are offered simple and effective ways to seek and receive help. Our studies have found that the vast majority of parents are capable of asking for and receiving help in ways that improve their and their child's situation. These experiences change the "ecology" of the problem. From here on, instead of the problem behavior flourishing in the hotbed of seclusion, which makes it swell and take root, the support network creates the conditions for the growth of a positive alternative and renewal of the child's sense of belonging.

Review and Application

- Note your tendency to keep a secret and maintain discretion over any other solution.

- Does the child pressure you not to tell anybody about the things they do? It is important to make it clear that from now on that is going to change.
- Seeking help is not weakness! Your child deserves parents who are willing and able to receive help instead of shutting down within themselves.
- The right to privacy is subject to its legitimate use. A child who uses privacy to take risks or hurt others or themselves forfeits that right.
- Sharing with grandparents, aunts/uncles, and close friends does not burden them. To the contrary, it honors them.
- Even modest help can be significant. Even help that is limited to a single house call, and a phone call proves that you are not alone anymore.
- When you are afraid the child will be harmed by feeling shame, make sure to create a situation where the supporter contacts the child with expressions of caring, love, belief in the child's capability, and willingness to help.
- If you say to yourselves "we have no one to help us!" this probably is more of a reflection of an entrenched habit and a mentality of seclusion than an actual situation.
- It is important to go over your contact list thoroughly, including people who live far away. No man is an island.

Chapter Four

Presence and Vigilance

To deal with the many challenges of parenting in the 21st century, parents need a sense of direction, an inner compass, a guiding principle. Otherwise, they cannot find their own way in the endless labyrinth of modern life, let alone lead their children to safety. Without a clear sense of direction, parents wander this way and that and add to the drift that constantly affects their children's lives. We coined the term, *parental presence,* to give parents a clear stance and sense of direction. A present parent gives the unmistakable message "I am here, and I am staying here! You cannot fire me or divorce me!"

Parental presence can be physical and mental. Physical presence is especially noticeable in the first years of life when the parent sees to all of their child's concrete and existential needs. Following infancy, physical presence gradually gives way to mental presence. When the transition from physical to psychological presence is made successfully, the parent continues to serve as a source of direction, values, security, and stability for the child. Now the parent is present in the child's heart, mind, and memory.

Parents accompany the child from afar or from closer up according to need. When they accompany their child from afar, they help the child develop independence and responsibility. If they pick up signs that something is wrong, they reassert more direct presence. We call this "parental vigilant care." Countless studies have proved that parental vigilant care is the most effective way to prevent risks of all kinds from early childhood to late adolescence. Since in our world temptations are mounting, the task of exercising vigilant care becomes the ultimate parental challenge. Therefore, the most important piece of advice we have for the parents of every child at every age is: learn how to be present. Dare to be vigilant.

Parental Vigilant Care

Vigilant care means staying on top of the situation, showing constant interest in what is happening with the child, being alert and attentive. This allows the parents to notice risks, act to prevent them, and take resolute action to rescue their child if and when needed. Vigilant care is also the ability to watch from the sidelines and see how the child manages on his or her own, as well as the willingness to act determinedly when the child is in trouble. The child needs to know the parent is watching, to make the vigilance really effective. The child thinks about the parent and knows that the parent is thinking about him or her as well. This silent dialogue between what is going through the parent's mind and what is going through the child's mind creates optimal conditions for growing up safely. The parent thereby accompanies the child, inspiring a sense security that lasts throughout childhood and adolescence and even beyond as can be seen by the following example.

> *New drivers are notoriously less safe drivers. Statistics show the risk to be greatest among boys*[8]*. Girls may have minor accidents, but they are usually not dangerous ones and often only require some body work. Boys, on the other hand, are involved in more serious accidents, particularly during their first year of independent driving. Therefore, we started a program for the parents of young drivers on how to maintain effective vigilance even though they are not next to the young driver. The secret is to create mental presence, which is a situation where the child is thinking about the parent because they know the parent is thinking about him or her.*
>
> *How is this done? Here is a small example: Before the youth goes out on the weekend, the mother makes a modest request, "Please, when you get to the destination, send me a short text message that you have arrived safely and another one before midnight so I can*

8 Shimshoni, Y., Farah, H., Lotan, T., Grimberg, E., Dritter, O., Musicant, O., Toledo, T., & Omer, H. (2015). Effects of parental vigilant care and feedback on novice driver risk. Journal of Adolescence, 38, 69-80.

go to sleep peacefully!" Some boys react impatiently to the mother's modest request. It is very important for the parents not to surrender to the boy's dismissive reaction and remember that the request is completely justified. The reason is twofold: the mother's request not only makes her calmer, but it also makes the boy think about his mother. When he fulfills her request, he thinks about her twice: when he gets to the destination and before midnight. Our studies have shown that when the parents exercise vigilant care, the young person's driving becomes much more cautious. We have also learned that when parents insist on their right to make such modest requests, the vast majority of young people (95%) comply. In one case, when a boy protested his mother's request, his father entered the picture and said, "Listen, dear son, when your mother doesn't sleep, I don't sleep, either! So, you are going to send those two messages!" And so it was.

In order to develop a good and effective stance of vigilant care, it is important to understand the big difference between vigilant care and things like spying and invasive intervention, which not only do not benefit the child (or the parent) but also can harm both the relationship and healthy development. Spying, or gathering information behind the child's back, is fundamentally different from vigilant care because it does not provide the child with presence. In addition, spying introduces an element of dishonesty which poses a risk of undermining the relationship. The damage becomes evident when the parent needs to act based on the information collected, or alternatively when the child discovers a parent was spying. A parent who tries to act based on spying information needs to lie to explain related actions. Even when the lie supposedly succeeds, an element of suspicion infects the relationship. Parents ask whether it is ever justified to actually check the child's actions (for example, to check whether the child is hiding drugs). Indeed, sometimes parents need to check in order to protect the child and the household. But the investigation can be carried out legitimately and openly—the opposite of spying. Thus, parents who discover their child is using drugs will tell the child openly that in light of that fact they are going to check the child's room if and when necessary. By doing so, the parents are not spying but exercising appropriately brave measures of vigilance to protect the child. Many parents need support in order to dare to act openly and legitimately, but once they have such support, even parents who were previously paralyzed dare to stand up and claim their parental status.

The effectiveness of vigilance is also undermined by cases of invasive intervention. Such intervention occurs when parents push themselves into their child's personal and intimate sphere or when they try to control areas where the child can function independently. A noteworthy example of the first kind of invasive intervention is reading their child's diary or electronic communications. A common example of the second kind is "helicopter parents," who hover incessantly over their children's lives and cannot let go even if there is no real sign of problem behavior by the child. Vigilance is undermined in these situations because the parental presence loses its legitimacy so that instead of the child accepting and welcoming the parents' position, they resist it increasingly strongly. Invasive vigilance has also been proven to harm the relationship between child and parent significantly.

In a workshop we held on parental vigilance concerning smoking and alcohol among children in grades eight and nine, several mothers admitted that they checked their children's bags behind their backs to see whether they had cigarettes. Some of the mothers got into trouble when they found "incriminating evidence."

Two of the mothers confronted their daughters that they knew for certain that they smoked. The girls denied it. The mothers said they knew because they "could tell." Both girls started to suspect that their mothers were going through their bags. They trapped their mothers by putting their bags on the chair in a certain way. When they came home and discovered their bags had been moved, they attacked their mothers, who ultimately admitted they had gone through them. This spying harmed the relationship, communication was blocked, and the mothers became even more helpless.

The desire to control the child and the child's life conditions in order to block any problem behavior completely and positively is not attainable and not desirable. Rather, parents can reduce risk significantly by giving their children the sense they are constantly in the parents' mind.

When parents ask us "how can we guarantee such a thing doesn't happen?" we tell them, "There is no guarantee, but this does not mean you are helpless!" On the contrary, the understanding that parental vigilance is expressed by your being present in the mind of the child rather than by control increases parents' legitimate influence. Vigilant care is a flexible process that becomes tighter or looser depending on the warning signals the parents pick up. We can speak of three levels of vigilant care: open attention, focused attention and unilateral measures.

Open Attention

Open attention is the most basic level of vigilant care. Most of the time parents are at that level because open attention provides the child with both independence and and a sense of being in the parents' mind at the same time. Parents maintain open attention when they show interest in what is happening, keep their eyes open, and stay updated but do not scrutinize too closely and do not intervene. By maintaining a respectful distance, the parent conveys to the child that the child is trusted and allowed to act independently. By showing they are thinking about the child and displaying constant positive interest they give the child the feeling that they are in the picture. Every parent can improve the ability to exercise open attention by cultivating the following skills:

Maintaining a Routine of Meeting Points

Parental presence occurs primarily by a series of contact points that are part of a routine, for instance, family meals. One of the problematic features of the drift in modern life is the gradual erosion of basic family occasions such as meals. There are countless reasons for the erosion of the routine of family meals. Parents are absent because of work, and children are absent because of social encounters, TV programs, or computer games. Gradually, family members develop habits such as grabbing something from the fridge or eating in their rooms in front of their screens. Not only do these habits undermine healthy eating, they also sabotage the family structure. Family meals have always been the hallmark of a functional family. For good reason. It turns out that families that eat together a few times a week have much less delinquency and substance abuse. Family meals strengthen parental presence in the child's mind. That presence grows not only during the meal itself but also prior to it from the very fact that the child knows that at a certain time they are expected at the table. This psychological presence helps immunize the child against drifting toward problematic temptations. The very fact that children know they are awaited reminds them that they have parents who care about them. Eating together is important even when it is not possible for the whole family to sit down at the table. Even just two family members sitting together contributes to the sense of belonging. The understanding that eating is done at the table and not in the bedroom in front of a screen also immunizes children against degeneration processes that are common today. Adolescents who develop the habit of eating in their rooms often enter a spiral of self-neglect. On the other hand, a parent who stands firmly against the bad habit of eating in the bedroom takes a step toward rehabilitating their children and their parenthood.

Meals are not the only events that uphold family routine. Any habit that provides points of encounter between parent and child or between family members can be the foundation for presence and basis for vigilant care. For instance, joint visits to grandparents, family vacations, trips, all strengthen a sense of belonging and provide a base of presence and vigilant care.

Another habit that enables parents to exercise open attention is the custom of accompanying children wherever they are going, such as driving them to friends, parties, or nights out. The drives are not only a parental service, but also create a sense of presence. The father of a teenage girl told her frankly, "It is important to me to drive you to meetings with friends. I trust you but I'm reassured if I know where you're hanging out!"

This father demonstrated he was not ashamed of being vigilant. All parents can ask themselves a number of questions to ascertain whether they are maintaining effective routine of contacts:

- Do I make sure to hold shared events such as meals, visits to grandparents, holidays, trips, and leisure activities?
- Do I insist that my children attend these events?
- Is there an erosion of the family atmosphere as a result of workload or family members going their separate ways?
- Has presence in shared spaces in the home declined, with each person spending more time in his or her own corner?
- Are there routine points of encounter between my children and me?

A parent who revives the practice of holding common events after abandoning the practice is reclaiming parenthood.

> *Ron, the divorced father of Karen, 13, recalled how after going through a period of depression after being fired he reinstated the routine of family gatherings that had declined while he was indisposed. Karen was a diehard Star Wars fan. Once she asked her father, "Why did you suddenly start demanding I come to every meal and every meeting with my grandparents and uncles?"*
>
> *He replied, "Because I was inspired by The Return of the Jedi that we saw a year ago. It reminded me that even someone who supposedly disappeared can make a big comeback! I, too, made a comeback after a difficult period when I was a little out of it." Karen went up to her father and embraced him warmly.*

Contacts with People in the Child's Environment

The principle of the sanctity of privacy has taken over our lives to such an extent that now we are sometimes ashamed to talk to our children's friends, get to know them, and have a simple conversation with them. Many adolescents shoot their parents furious looks when they "embarrass" them by striking up small talk with their friends. The parents, for their part, quickly fall in line because "embarrassing" their children is the last thing they want to be accused of. However, parental fear and shame are not only unjustified but also damaging. Getting to know our children's friends is our duty. At the very least, parents should know the names of the friends and be able to turn to them with a question or request if necessary. It also helps to know where they live. It is not too much to aspire to have a few of their phone numbers in the parents' contact list. Parents ask themselves whether by doing so they are not showing their child they do not trust them 100%. Actually, trusting 100% is not a good idea. Children grow up better with a little less trust. Every child would benefit from their parents' trust not being blind trust but rather realistic trust.

Following are a number of statements parents can say to themselves or their child in order to insist on their right to know the child's friends:

> "It is my duty to know who you run around with!"

"It is important for me to know your friends. They are an important part of your life so they are also an important part of my life!"

"Everyone who comes to my house is my guest! I'm not going to be a stranger to anyone who visits me!"

"When your friends come over, I welcome them personally, and if they stay, I serve them light refreshments!"

These statements help parents avoid the problematic situation in which the child's friends are off-limits to them. The very fact that a child says to the parent "it's none of your business!" is a warning sign that requires tightening supervision. Asking the child (and the teacher) who their friends are at school provides parents with an initial toehold in order to maintain proper vigilance.

Open house at school and PTA meetings are a good opportunity to catch up on this. Parent days are also an opportunity to expand the network of contacts to include some of the parents of the child's classmates. It is rare for another parent to reject an address such as: "I understand your daughter Ricky spends a lot of time with my daughter Dorothy. Here is my phone number. I'd be happy to have yours so we can talk if necessary!"

When parents dare to move out of their tendency to isolate themselves, they quickly discover that other parents are willing and even eager for contact. By "coming out" as responsible and vigilant parents, we help others do the same.

Parents who create points of contact with a number of figures in the child's environment increase their capacity to pick up danger signs and intervene early to prevent negative developments. By way of contrast, parents who are disconnected from the figures surrounding the child necessarily have a limited field of vision. Some parents might be averse to seeking help from others in knowing what is happening with their child. They might see it as proof of distrust between their child and them, or they might fear that creating contacts is like setting up a "radar network" to spy on the child. It is important to bear in mind that creating contact with the people surrounding the child is done out in the open. The parent tells the child openly: "I need to know who your friends are!" "I need to know what is happening with you at school!"

Some parents say, "I don't need others because I know instantly if something bad is happening to my child!" This position is arrogant. Even the most sensitive parent will sometimes be surprised by things happening to their child without their noticing.

Open Dialogue

One of the best means of effective vigilance is having open and direct dialogue with the child. Parents differ in their ability to have such dialogue, but some basic principles can help every parent improve.

The first principle is that merely conducting a conversation in a good atmosphere is more important than the information the parent manages to draw out of the child. There are a few reasons for this. When the parent and child discuss an area of life that has the potential of trouble the parent becomes more present in the child's mind, when that kind of trouble arises. For instance, if they are talking about parties and the parent asks what the child will do if they are offered alcohol or drugs, the child will probably think about the parent if that actually happens. This kind of psychological accompaniment is one of the best means to protect the child from temptation. In addition, having a conversation in a good atmosphere increases the chance that if the child will willingly go to their parent for help when confronted with trouble.

To create a positive atmosphere that enables meaningful dialogue, the parent must avoid preaching, displaying anger, or interrogation. Preaching has a negative impact even if the parent's position is justified. What is the difference between preaching and expressing the parent's position in an effective way? Preaching is characterized by repetition and an invasive tone. Children exposed to preaching learn to immunize themselves against it.

Anger and threats pose a significant barrier to open dialogue. Parents know this well. When parents are asked why their children don't share problems with them, they answer, "Because they're afraid I'll be angry!"

How should parents react when they find out their child is involved in problem behavior? After all, the parent is not a skilled psychologist who can respond with impartial restraint and a nod of understanding to even the most shocking disclosures. Nonetheless, parents can improve their reactions, for instance, if they internalize the principle of striking while the iron is cold! A possible reaction when the parent finds out a child was involved in something problematic is to say, "It is not easy for me to hear what you told me. I'm sure you can understand that. Let me take it in and think about it, and then we'll talk about it again."

Surprisingly, such a reaction has greater impact than expressing deep shock, let alone when the shock comes with anger and threats. But parents are human. They cannot be expected to react "by the book" when they are dumbfounded. Luckily, even a parent who responds with an outburst can improve and correct a reaction and improve the chances of a constructive dialogue in the future. For instance, the parent can go back to the child and say, "I screamed at you when I found out what you did because I was astonished and shocked. But now I want to talk about it in a different state of mind. Let's sit down quietly and discuss how to prevent such things happening again!" This reaction reopens the subject that was shut down by the parent's outburst.

Another obstacle to opening a dialogue with the child is interrogation, which is the attempt to extract from the child incriminating information or a confession. The attempt to interrogate often leads to the opposite reaction: children will entrench themselves in their refusal and resolutely avoid providing parents with the coveted information or confession. Like in the case of preaching, the key to a constructive dialogue is striking the right tone and avoiding invasive repetitions or clamorous demands to disclose the truth. If during the conversation a clear indication of problematic behavior arises, the parent can tell the child, "I would like you to think about how you're going to tell me what happened. Let's not do it now because first I want us both to calm down. Let's talk about it again this evening."

Later, when conditions for a calm conversation are better, the parent should sit with the child and say, "Let's start over. Tell me exactly what happened, and together let's figure out the best way to solve this." If the child insists on refusing to tell what happened, the parent can say. "I'm sorry you don't want to tell me. I know what I know, and I'll act accordingly. I will tighten my supervision and from now on follow things closely."

It is worth creating comfortable conditions to facilitate a constructive dialogue. It is important to set aside the time and find a suitable place to do so. It also helps to announce it in advance. For instance, "I want to talk to you about your trip to Atlantic City. It's the first time you're going on a trip alone with friends, and I want to go over some important points with you first. I suggest we meet in the living room tonight after you get back from basketball practice." The fact that the parent announces the meeting in advance and sets a time and place creates good opening conditions. In contrast, the attempt to have a rushed conversation or to talk when tempers are high is doomed to failure.

One of the main goals of a conversation initiated by the parent is to construct a shared script for a situation with a problematic potential such as a dance party, a trip with friends, or exposure to harmful substances. Parents should prepare for these conversations in advance. A good way to do so is for both parents to have a preliminary conversation in an attempt to reach a joint position. When both parents can agree on a joint message, chances of a positive reaction by the child increase. The conversation with the child should begin with a direct statement such as, "I want to talk to you about cigarettes (or pornography, drugs, unprotected sex, etc.). How do you think you will respond if you are offered or exposed to them?"

If the child cooperates, the goal should be to build a joint script, e.g., the parent and child together envision a situation of facing temptation or social pressure to try and come up with a desirable response. Often, though, the child does not cooperate or does so only with irritation or a dismissive comment like, "Oh, Mom, I know how to protect myself!"

The way to maintain the positive effect of the conversation despite the attempt to dismiss it is to say to the child, "I'm glad to hear you know how to protect yourself, but it is important for me to tell you what Dad and I think about this."

If the child is willing to listen, the parents can tell them briefly what their position and concerns are. If the child still resists, the parents can say to them, "We have not finished this conversation. and we're not interested in continuing in a bad atmosphere. We are still going to look for a solution to make this subject clear to all of us."

One way to make sure the parents' position is conveyed effectively despite the child's demonstrated resistance is to be helped by a supporter. For instance, a grandfather, uncle, or family friend can invite the child to a conversation about their parents' expectation and concern. A good conversation about a problematic subject by a supporter of the parents is a preferred alternative to attempting to have the conversation directly, if and when the child resists.

Focused Attention

When signs emerge that the child is getting in trouble, such as cutting school, disappearing in the evenings, lying, or developing dubious friendships, it is not enough for parents to stay at the level of open attention. They must raise their level of vigilance and check the problematic areas close up. It is important to remember: one must dare to act openly and avowedly. The child must feel that their parents are supervising them more closely and know why they found it necessary to do so.

Zara, the mother of Eli, 13, divorced Chaim a year ago. Following the divorce, she moved to another city, and Eli made new friends there. Eli lived with her, and his father came to visit him twice a week. To make Eli's adjustment easier, Zara gave him more freedom than usual. Eli started to adjust, and since he was a very social boy, he quickly made friends with kids from the neighborhood.

Slowly, concerning signs began to appear. He started to come home late and would give evasive answers.

Zara initiated some frank talks, which took place in a friendly atmosphere, but the situation did not improve. After she found out that Eli had lied to her about going out with a friend, she decided it was time to tighten her supervision.

Her first step was to coordinate her position with Chaim, who, she was happy to find, supported her even though his natural inclination was to give Eli more freedom than Zara would have liked to. When Eli visited his father, he was surprised to discover he had invited his mother to his new house. They both sat down with Eli in the living room, and Zara began: "There were a few times lately when you came home very late, and once you even lied to me. I spoke to your dad, and we decided that our new living arrangements have confused us all. We decided it was time to put things in order. From now on, I'm going to ask you every night what your plans are for the next day. I will ask you what you will be doing, where you're going, and who you're going with. I'm going to ask you for your friends' names and phone numbers. I'm going to report to Dad on a regular basis."

Eli protested against the demand to give his friends' details. Chaim, who had coordinated with Zara about this point, answered, "It's a very small request. If everything goes well, Mom won't bother you or anybody else. But if anything concerning happens, we will call anyone who can help us."

Eli was very surprised by the coordination between his parents. This signaled to him that he had crossed several of their red lines. In the following weeks, the new routine took hold.

The announcement to the child that the parent is going to ask for information every time the child goes out—who, what, where and until when—is the core of the transition to the "focused attention" level of vigilant care. Some parents are uncomfortable about the questioning process because it departs from the atmosphere of open dialogue they would prefer to maintain. This might make them feel uncomfortable and cause them to ask their questions without conviction. This discomfort means the parents feel wrong about close supervision. They feel this conveys mistrust. Therefore, it is important to understand that the demand for simple information (who, what, where and until when) is very modest. After all, we are talking about children who have already "faked" or given different worrisome signals. In these cases, the focused questions are necessary. Parents who understand that by demanding simple and basic information they are doing a critical job will do so with a sense of inner peace. It is precisely the willingness to ask that gives the best answer to the trust question. Now the trust that they give their child will be realistic trust rather than blind trust. Children benefit only from reasonable trust. Blind trust hurts the child twice: first, because giving such trust exposes them to unnecessary temptations, and second, because when the child violates the full (and blind) trust the parents give them, parents are twice as disappointed. Therefore blind trust both raises the risk and worsens the relationship.

Parents often ask what they should do if the child refuses to answer. Our answer is twofold. First, when the parents insist, the vast majority of children answer, even if they do so halfheartedly. Second, if the child still refuses, the parent can say quietly but forcefully, "Then, you can't go out."

This simple statement seems mysterious to many parents, who ask themselves how they can stick to that message. Parents' objection to the child going out is expressed in three steps: the parents inform the child of the restriction against going out, the parents do not give the child money (not just for that day but at all), and if the child still goes out even though forbidden and not given money, the parents look for the child. If the child defiantly says. "I'm going out anyway," it is important to explain, "We can't stop you by force, but if you go out, we are going to look for you. We are not going to give up on you!"

When parents tighten supervision to the level of focused attention regarding school matters, they make sure to inquire about homework, tests, and attendance. They stay in touch not only with the homeroom teacher but also with other teachers, after-school instructors, and counselors. They show the child they notice any change in behavior. Raising the level of supervision is a step where parents' presence is visible. This extracts the parent from the state of effacement they were in before. The child has an experience of "the return of the parent" after a period of dimming presence. We wish to emphasize that even if the child resists, deep inside, the change is welcomed. A child who takes risks needs a safety net. When parents go back to supervising, the child is liberated from the feeling of walking alone at the edge of an abyss.

Unilateral Measures

The highest level of supervision is expressed by measures meant to protect and extract the child from any entanglement or scrape. At this stage, parents are not satisfied by talk but move to action. For instance, they call the children they have put on a phone tree, physically go to where the child is, deny the child access to things that can result in harm (such as the car or a credit card), and in some cases, limit the child's personal rights. The parents' activity at this level of supervision does not depend on the child's agreement. These are measures the parents take even if the child resists. The justification is obvious: the parents are acting to rescue their child.

The Phone Tree

Parents' willingness to call a large number of people in the child's environment when the child disappears or refuses to come home on time creates a deep change in their status, knowledge level, and ability to provide their child with a feeling of supervision. Parents who make an extensive phone tree of the telephone numbers of their child's friends undergo a baptism of fire that infuses them with strength and courage. What used to seem impossible to them starts to seem possible. In order to decide whether it is befitting to prepare for this measure, parents might ask themselves:

- Does my child lie to me?
- Has my child been hiding any actions from me lately?
- Does my child try to prevent me from knowing his or her friends?
- Does my child disappear for longer times or go out a lot at night without reporting to me?
- Have I recently picked up worrisome signals about pastimes with friends?

A positive answer to these questions indicates that the child is trying to establish areas in life that are off-limits to parents. Sometimes, that desire is legitimate, for instance when it comes to intimate relationships. But hanging out with friends in unacceptable hours or places does not fall into that category. In this area, parents need to stay on top of the situation. The child's attempt to shake parents off constitutes a clear warning sign.

Is the phone tree a drastic measure, recommended only in the case of children who have already gotten into serious trouble? We estimate that at least half of all parents would benefit significantly if they used the phone tree at least once. When parents go through the process of phone tree usage, they change themselves, their capacity, and their status. They stop being parents who can be ignored and reclaim their initiative. Therefore, we view the preparation and use of a phone tree as an act that even typical parents should try and not only parents of children who have gotten into serious trouble.

In broad usage of a phone tree, parents call as many of the child's friends as possible, talk to them, and ask to speak to one of their parents. Many parents are surprised at this and ask why they should do it if they can simply make direct contact with their child over their cell phone. True, parents can begin by calling their child on the cell phone and asking them where they are and why they aren't back yet. If the child answers and is willing to come right back or let the parents come pick them up, there is no need to call other children. But if the child brushes them off, talks back, provides vague information, or rejects the parents' request with various excuses, the parent can say, "I don't accept that; if you don't keep agreements, it is my duty to take action."

The parent waits for the child's response, giving another chance to end the unauthorized activity. Some parents say that this will most likely be the scenario so they don't need the phone tree. This is exactly where the advantage of preparation comes in. If parents know what measures they're going to take, they convey a quiet determination that is immeasurably more persuasive than threatening to take measures without having prepared for them in advance. In fact, parents who do not prepare and make a general threat to take measures tend to respond poorly later on, for instance, by shouting, threatening, preaching, or meting out severe punishments that make the situation even worse. Advance preparation is the best guarantee of self-control. The child who sees parents who are determined and self-controlled responds differently from a child who feels parents drifting into an impulsive reaction. Therefore, preparing a phone tree offers the best chances for an episode to end well even if the parents do not actually need to make the calls.

The very collection process is a step that strengthens the parents and keeps them on top of the situation. There are several ways to collect the information. The basic way is to say to the child simply, "I need to know the names and phone numbers of your friends. Could you please give them to me?"

For many parents, even this simple question is an insurmountable obstacle. These parents feel uncomfortable and think it is invasive to ask a child for this information. Or, they simply fear the child will refuse. That is precisely why preparation is such an important process. It encourages parents to scrutinize themselves and confront the fears that so severely restrict their parenting. If parents avoid as simple an action as asking the child about friends, they risk giving up their ability to supervise and thereby abandoning their child to temptations and questionable influences.

Another approach is to use the classroom list or other contact lists. Sometimes, parents have to approach the school, other parents, or a youth counselor to get several more contacts. These are significant actions in their own right. Parents can also address the child's friends who visit their home or other parents at school events. Here, too, the simple request, "Could you please give me your cell phone number? I'll use it only if necessary, I promise not to bother you!" is a basic act of parental presence. Parents who overcome their initial discomfort and turn to other children or parents to get contact details of people in their child's environment achieve the capacity and courage to supervise.

A significant phone tree will include a number of children and adults. It is not rare for parents to reach 20 different people. The purpose of calling the phone tree is not necessarily to get the child home immediately but to demonstrate determined presence. The calling can also be carried out the next day, for instance. if it was too late to call strangers. In this case, parents can tell the people they call, "My son disappeared last night and only got home at dawn. I'm very worried about that! That's why I'm calling you and other people who my son is in touch with. I'd be very grateful if you could give me a minute or two of your time!"

In every conversation, parents must identify themselves, say why they're calling, and ask for modest help. For instance: "I'm very worried my daughter didn't come home, I don't know where she is. Could you help me?" After this opening, parents will try to have a short conversation. If they are talking to a child who sees their child regularly, such as a classmate, the parent can add what we call "the million-dollar request," which is this, "I have a little favor to ask you. Tomorrow when you see my daughter, could you tell her that I called you because I was very worried?"

Experience shows that about half of the children do tell the child that the parents called (if only to laugh at them). These messages have a profound significance for parental presence. Parents are actually showing their child, "We were here, we were there, and we were elsewhere." That is the core of vigilance: proving to the child that the parents do not give up on the child.

When ending the conversation with the child who was on the list, it is advisable to ask for one of the child's parents to come to the phone. The parents' goal is to make contact with at least some of the parents of the children in their child's social circle. This connection might be extremely important later on. It is important to explain to the parent on the line that the measure is being taken out of deep parental concern. Such an explanation frequently elicits a positive response from the other side. If the other parent responds in an encouraging way, it is worth trying to set up a meeting. An alliance between parents as a result of a phone tree call sometimes leads to significant gains as far as protecting their children. In two cases we handled, groups of parents created in this way managed to break up drug distribution networks that were operating freely at school. In another case, the parents' alliance put an end to alcohol parties that had already become a norm among a whole group of seventh graders.

Numerous parents have told us that use of a phone tree changed their and their children's lives. Parents of a 14-year-old boy who started to get in trouble told us, "If only we had been aware of this possibility when our older daughter got in trouble, everything could have been different! But maybe it's not too late!"

The parents' role does not end with calling the phone tree. Parents must prepare for the almost inevitable confrontation that will happen when children find out their parents called their friends. Here, too, the preparation itself fortifies the parents. In the case of using a phone tree, a furious reaction from the child can be expected because the parents shattered a sacred taboo of the teenage value system: the taboo against calling their friends. When parents dare to violate this taboo, they are telling the child: "You are too important to us for us to just sit there when you get in trouble!" By doing so, they are reclaiming their parenthood. Some parents feel very proud after calling a phone tree. It is indeed a considerable achievement. A parent who has gone through such an experience will not back down easily even when their child makes a scene.

The parents' goal the day after the telephone calls is to avoid being drawn into an escalation when they face their child's assault. The optimal initial response is to absorb the child's rage quietly. When the child stops shouting, it is the parents' turn to say simply and quietly, "We are not interested in calling anybody, and we won't if you just tell us where you are and come home on time."

It is advisable to avoid a threatening or preaching tone. If the child goes back to attacking and threatening, the parent should be quiet and finally say calmly: "If you are not willing to fulfill my simple request, then I have no choice but to act as a loving and responsible parent."

At this point, it is advisable to end the meeting unilaterally. Do not expect the child to agree. A telephone round is a unilateral measure necessitated by the parental duty to protect the child against clear dangers. No social norm of privacy stands above that duty.

Parents who prepare for a confrontation in this way can show restraint and self-control. In all the cases in which we have been involved, there was not a single case in which a parent who prepared was drawn into an escalation. The conversation may have sometimes ended with by the child's slamming the door, but the parents stood their ground.

The child cannot be expected to simply fall into line after one or two such rounds of calling. On the contrary, most children will change only gradually and partially.

However, a deep change occurs in the parents. The phone-tree approach opens to the parents options that were previously closed to them. An extensive set of calls deeply changes the ecology in which the child's problematic behavior flourished. Instead of paralyzed parents, the child now meets committed and confident parents. The parents' self-control is contagious. It is very hard to keep yelling at parents who stand their ground calmly. Slowly, the child begins to appreciate the parents. Instead of hysterical or easy-to-ignore parents , the child now meets parents who are ready, responsible, and devoted to their job. The child also finds that their parents receive support and legitimacy. These are completely new conditions in terms of the child's problem behavior. The consequences for the child are gradual but unmistakable: many studies prove that the risk level gradually lowers.

Presence on the Ground

The parent's willingness to go to the place where the child spends time or to meet different parties that are connected with the problem behavior sends a strong message of concern, care, and daring. Care for the child is especially noteworthy when the parent arrives to rescue the child from trouble, for instance if the child is under arrest at the police station, found drunk or high, or detained at school because of violent behavior. The parent should first of all express concern, both to the child and to those around the child. Demonstrating anger, threatening punishment, or trying to grab the child physically can be very harmful. The correct reaction is a combination of restraint with a show of willingness to take the necessary measures to prevent the situation from recurring. Now the parent conveys the message, "I am here to help my child and to prevent this from happening again." This position embodies the essence of vigilance: protection and prevention. Their concern puts the parent on their child's side. Resolute vigilance puts the parent between the child and the risk.

Our main advice to parents in this situation is: express genuine concern for your child's predicament, but also respect the people around the child and listen to what these people say. And above all, control yourselves! This is not the time to discipline your child, let alone scold other people.

If parents follow these guidelines, their appearance at the site can be a powerful event that changes their status, their relationship with their child's environment, and the child's risk level. Following are a couple of typical situations:

> *(1) An 11-year-old boy told his parents he was sleeping over at a friend's house even though they told him he must come home by 9 PM. The father called the friend's mother and told her his son had permission to visit but not to sleep over. He told her he was worried because his son had started coming home late and sometimes his parents didn't know where he was. He told her he was coming to pick up his son soon. When he got there, the father told the friend that his son could sleep over another time but not this time because he did not get permission in advance. Later, the parents sat down with their son to work out how he could get permission to sleep over at his friend's. They emphasized that they would not accept any attempt to face them with a fait accompli.*

> *(2) A mother found out that her 12-year-old daughter had lied to her and said she was doing homework at her friend's house. It turned out that she had agreed with several girlfriends to go to a movie her mother had forbidden her from seeing because she didn't think it was appropriate for her age. A phone call to one of the friends' mothers identified what theater the girls had gone to. The mother went to the theater, talked to the manager, and said her daughter was in there without permission. The mother told him respectfully that she had come out of concern for her daughter. The manager offered to accompany her into the auditorium. The mother found her daughter and pulled her out of the movie. On the way home, she told her: "I don't want to talk to you now because neither of us is calm. Let's talk about it again this evening. We need to find a way to prevent this from happening again!"*

In both of these cases, the same principle is at work: The parent personally arrived at the site of the problem behavior or made direct contact with the people around the child. In both cases, the parents took action that indicated tightening supervision. Traditional punishments, such as grounding or forbidding use of screens, do not contribute whatsoever to improving the situation. However, for many children the very supervision feels like a punishment of sorts. But this kind of punishment is another cup of tea. It is probably the best and most generous "punishment" that a child at risk may experience.

Conclusion

Vigilance is a parental position manifested by a rising continuum of involvement: expressing interest, creating points of contact and connection, questioning, checking, and intervening. The amount of vigilance is determined by the warning signals parents pick up. Thus, when things are going well, the parent supervises less, and the child receives maximum freedom that safely promotes greater independence. Under those circumstances the child will be able to develop an active social life, keep track of time, and develop responsibility. When worrying signs start to appear, parents question the child directly and pointedly. In this way, parents give the child the feeling they are involved in the child's events. When a child has already gotten into a problematic situation, parents actively intervene. One way is by making phone contact with everyone surrounding the child, resisting the problem behavior without escalating, and when needed, personally coming to wherever the child is located. Countless studies prove that parental vigilance is key to reducing risk in our children's lives. Vigilance works by conveying a continuous experience of psychological presence: children feel they are in their parents' minds, and that the parents are in their mind. This creates an experience of being accompanied, even when the parents are far away.. These are the optimal conditions for the child to internalize the parents' vigilance. In this way the child develops self-vigilance.

Review and Application

- Create points of encounter and spend time together with the child, such as meals, driving, shared events.

- Contact people surrounding the child. Find out who the child's friends are and make sure the friends know who you are. Also contact teachers, counselors and other children's parents.
- It is important to initiate a simple and direct conversation on potentially problematic subjects. Talk to the child about cigarettes, alcohol, pornography, unprotected sex, and undesirable computer or cell phone use. Even if the child does not provide incriminating information, the conversation is meaningful because it increases your presence.
- Do not spy! Do not read the child's cell phone communications! Dare to supervise openly!
- Vigilance differs from anxious or invasive parental behavior. When there are no signs of risk, supervision should be reduced to the level of open attention and should not be raised to a tighter level.
- The best way to raise the level of vigilance is to inform the child that in light of the concerning events that occurred you are going to ask questions and keep a closer eye on things.
- Tightening vigilance differs from punishment and is more effective than any punishment.
- Connect with supporters in order to supervise better. The more connected you are, the more effective and legitimate the supervision will be.
- Learn how to make and use a phone tree. There is nothing as powerful for fortifying your parental standing.
- Don't be unnerved by the child protesting or claiming you are violating his or her privacy. In the face of problematic discoveries, it is necessary to reduce privacy rights.
- The child's room is not the holy of holies. When children use their room dangerously, it is your duty to go in and check, informing them of your decision even if the exact time of the visit is not known to them.

- When children improve their behavior, tell them that your level of trust has risen and lower the amount of supervision accordingly.
- Increasing vigilance sometimes feels uncomfortable or embarrassing. Remind yourself that it is a critical part of your parenting.
- Many children use loaded words like "privacy," or "shame" to deter you from carrying out your supervision. Listen quietly, and insist on your right to protect your child.
- Vigilance is not control, but it is an important key to the child being able to develop self-control.

Chapter Five

The Loving Limit

Setting limits is a common term in child-rearing. Indeed, children must learn what lines they are not allowed to cross. But effective limits are more than just anonymous prohibitions backed by sanctions. The child must feel that behind every limit is a caring and conscientious person. This provides the child with an experience of a loving limit. When small children get close to a forbidden place and hear from their parents the word "no!" in a warning tone of voice, they experience not only the prohibition but also the personal presence of the person imposing it. This is evident when their eyes meet. This meeting can persist for a long moment. This is a significant moment, in which the child considers whether to accept the prohibition. Children who accept the limit are on their way to internalizing it. If a child continues moving toward the forbidden place, the process of imposing the limit continues. For instance, the parent might pick up and take the child away from the forbidden place. Now the child is not only limited but also held. That is the secret of the loving limit: the parent is the limit. Parents are not merely "setting a limit" for the child. They are the limit.

The limit experience goes both ways: Not only does the child feel the limit and need it, but so does the parent. For the parent, setting the limit means "here I stand!" Setting a limit is like fixing an anchor to the seafloor. When parents find their limit, or the place where they stand firm, they stop being confused or feeling harassed. This can be seen clearly in the family routine. A parent who decides that the family sits down for dinner at 7 PM creates a clear and stable point in the family life, which provides everyone with a beginning sense of structure and belonging.

Between Limit and Power Struggle

Being caught in power struggles creates an experience of anger, exhaustion, and futile repetition. In this sense, power struggles are the complete opposite of meaningful limits. The typical signs of power struggles are

a. Power struggles are characterized by "ping-pong" interactions; for instance, the parent demands and the child refuses, the parent demands again and the child refuses again, and so on, until reaching exhaustion or flareup.

b. In a power struggle the parent seeks full and immediate obedience. The basic statement is "you will do what I say!"

c. Power struggles are characterized by a sense of threat: The parent feels threatened by potential loss of authority through failure to prevail, and the child feels threatened by loss of independence in surrendering.

d. Even though the parent enters the power struggle to demonstrate inequality between parent and child, the result is that both sides act in similar ways. It is no wonder that a parent caught in a power struggle is said to have "stooped to the child's level."

The experience of a meaningful limit is very different:

a. The parent is not saying to the child "you will do what I say!" but rather "I will do what I say!" A particularly effective way to communicate this message is in the first-person plural: "We will do what we say!"

b. Instead of entering into a ping-pong match with the child, the parent takes a deep breath and prepares to stick to the imposed limit

c. Parents break free from the sense of threat; they understand that their status depends on what they do and not on the child's reaction.

d. Instead of repeating the demand for automatic obedience, the parent reinforces the limit by persistence, support, and legitimacy.

Shepherd, the father of Max (2), spoke about his confrontation with his son. When Shepherd was feeding Max in a high chair, Max purposely threw a piece of bread on the floor. Shepherd said "no!" and put the bread back on the high chair tray. Max took the piece of bread and threw it down again defiantly. Shepherd put the bread back on the tray, repeated the admonition, waved his finger at the boy and glared at him. Shepherd said that at that moment he had the feeling that if he didn't obtain his son's obedience, he would be planting the seeds for a future criminal.

Luckily the mother, Ella, was watching the scene from the sidelines. She picked up Max, distracted him, and put an end to the power struggle.

Shepherd was disappointed that Ella did not back him up, but after a discussion, they agreed that if it happened again, one of the parents would simply end the power struggle by taking Max out of his seat. Thus, both parents decided on a clear limit: "We stop letting you sit at the table when you throw food on the floor!"

This daily experience illustrates the difference between a power struggle and a constructive limit. Instead of the futile power struggle, the parents decided on a position, planned their joint response, and focused on their own actions.

Two Kinds of "No!"

Sometimes, parents feel as if all they ever say is "no!" "enough!" and "stop it!"

No-Chatter

To emphasize the exhausting repetition and ineffectiveness of incessant interdictions, we call this "no-chatter." At the end of the day, the parents feel harassed, exhausted and hoarse, from their countless efforts to warn, demand, and discipline. It is especially difficult when the parent is trying to deal with a child with attention and hyperactivity disorder. Such children need constant new stimulation. Their basic experience is of a constant stream of stimulation, distracting their attention and leading them to reach their hands out in ever-changing directions. These children "dance" to a tune whose refrain is "now!" "now!" "now!" The parent who tries to deal with one or sometimes several such children, needs to repeatedly cry "no!" "no!" "no!" The parent's prohibitions and demands are added to the noise of the child's incessant stimulation, to create a sweeping merry-go-round of shrill experiences. Our goal is to change the parental "no" and imbue it with a dimension which, instead of intensifying the deluge of events, will create a balancing and stabilizing effect. We wish to change the "no-chatter" into a "no-anchor."

No-Anchors

"No-anchors" are limits that are characterized by the parents' readiness to stand behind them and persist in their implementation by continuous attention, systematic follow-up and, in case of need, mobilizing their supporters for aid and validation. By means of a "no-anchor", parents manifest decisive readiness to stand against pressure. Naturally, "no-anchors" should be much less frequent and better thought out than "no-chatter." We suggest that parents produce a "no-anchor" at most once a week.

The first stage in producing a no-anchor is determining in advance what problem behavior to focus on. The parent does not shoot from the hip but considers, decides and carries out a pre-considered decision. It is even more effective if both parents decide together, e.g., "This week we are going to focus on the bad habit of playing with the cell phone while getting ready for school in the morning." Even if one parent leaves for work early and is not present at this time, both parents can make it clear to the child that the decision about the cell phone was mutual.

The second stage in producing a "no anchor" is to tell it to the child in advance, "We decided we will no longer let you use your cell phone in the morning. You can only turn it on when you leave for school!" If the child ignores this request and turns on the phone the next day contrary to the parents' decision, the parent who is present can remind the child, "We cannot accept this; we will talk it over and decide what to do about your violation of the limit we have established" At night, one of the parents (preferably the other one) should demand the child's cell phone and say: "You will get it back tomorrow, after you finish getting ready and leave for school!" Now the child will feel that the parental limit has depth, as expressed by the parents' mutual coordination and consistency.

"No-anchors" differ from "no-chatter" in several ways:

- They are special occasions, in which the parental limit relates to the subject the parents decided to focus on that week.
- They are not shots from the hip like "no-chatter."
- The parents inform the child in advance what limit they have decided to enforce.
- If and when the child violates the limit, the parent tells the child they will consider their next steps and come back to the subject later (strike while the iron is cold).
- The parents stick to the limit they set not only that week but for the following weeks. It might be better not to move on to a new subject until the previous limit has been habituated.

It is best for the decision about the "no-anchor" to be made by both parents. If that is not possible, such as if the parents are divorced, it would be helpful to recruit support from another family member, e.g., a grandfather who talks to the child and verbally supports the mother's (or father's) decision on the subject in question.

Strategic Depth

The manner of enforcing the no-anchor provides the established limit with "strategic depth." Whereas previously the limit was superficial and randomly set in the heat of the moment, now it is planned, marked, backed up, and ongoing.

Producing "no-anchors" gradually changes parents' behavior as a whole, well beyond the selected subject. That is because the parents feel more in control, more planful, better coordinated, and more persistent.

Changed Atmosphere

The child, too, begins to experience the parent differently. Now, the child knows that the parent is capable of producing another kind of "no."

The production of "no-anchors" significantly reduces the parents' "no-chatter" as a result of the parent sensing the ineffectiveness of constant chatter. This changes the family's feeling of chaos. Whereas in the past the "family noise" was the product of the child's impulsive actions ("now!" "now!" "now!"), multiplied by the parents' shrill answers ("no!" "no!" "no!"), this is no longer the case: The child may continue to chirp "now now now," but the parents' reaction is like a long bass "noooooooooooooooooooo!" This changes the atmosphere and gradually also the child's behavior.

This process has proven to be effective even in especially difficult cases. The parents' ability to set "no-anchor" limits makes a positive change in parents' behavior, alleviating their feeling of harassment and ameliorating the child's problematic behavior.

The Announcement

An announcement is a structured action designed to serve as a sort of rite of passage between the way things were and the way they are going to be. Rites of passage are festive and formal events that are validated by the environment and mark the end of a previous status and the commencement of a new one. Examples are confirmations, bar mitzvahs, weddings, divorces, signing contracts, graduations, and so on. In all of these cases, the change of status is marked by a special event at which not only the people involved are present but also others, who affirm and validate the change. The reason for the formal atmosphere and involvement of witnesses who add validation to the rite of passage is the desire to draw a boundary of awareness that enables those involved to think, feel and act differently.

Many parents frequently inform their children of a change of their policy toward problem behavior. Such announcements often fail because they normalize ignoring them. One of the common explanations for the weakness of statements of policy change is that they are "toothless." The presumption is that if there are sanctions, the limit is effective, but if there are not, the limit dissipates. This is a partial and even harmful understanding. It is partial because it ignores additional critical elements of every act of setting a limit, such as: clarity, legitimacy, and decisiveness. It is harmful because automatic thinking that tends toward sanctions leads to escalation and sometimes delegitimization.

Sanctions

Sanctions can lead to escalation of a power struggle because the statement "I will show you!" that goes with threatening a sanction invites the automatic response, "I will show *you*!" This sets the stage for a greater power struggle, with each side trying to get the other to blink first.

Sanctions can also lead to delegitimization because most of the old punishments are no longer acceptable. In many cases, tightening sanctions brings parents closer to the use of physical force even if that was not their initial intention. That is because punishments make the child increasingly angry to the point of throwing a fit. Parents then find themselves in a dilemma: to allow the child to continue the fit or use force to stop it. In many cases parents themselves are also alarmed by the escalation in which they find themselves trapped. Thus, exclusive faith in sanctions undermines parents' resolve and worsens the helplessness it sought to relieve.

However, we do not consider every punishment illegitimate. No society can exist without punishments. But punishments should be used judiciously. For instance, a school that decides that if a student cheats on a test the test will be disqualified, is using punishment legitimately. The purpose of this punishment is not only to change the behavior of the unruly student but also to set a norm for all of the students. Such punishments are necessary for the functioning of any system. But even though punishments are important in certain situations, the parental limit does not need to rely on them. To the contrary, the parental limit relies primarily on the willingness to send the determined message, "Here we stand!"

Formulation of an Announcement

An announcement is a semi-formal statement the parents deliver to the child together, at their initiative, at a suitable time and place. The announcement is not delivered in the heat of an argument or in immediate response to a problematic behavior. It is given at a different time, such as when the child is in their room after finishing the day's work. It is necessary to prepare in order to deliver the announcement correctly.

The preparation process should seek to define a limited number of problematic behaviors the parents decide to resist with all their might. The main subjects the announcement focuses on are violence, behavior that hurts members of the household (such as theft, humiliation, and tyranny), or behavior that harms the child (such as alcohol, disappearing for long hours, and not going to school). These subjects are relatively easy to define. In contrast, vaguer issues, such as insolence or disobedience in general, although they are important, are not suitable for an announcement. The reason is that the difficulty to judge whether a given incident constitutes crossing the red line ("Is that really insolence or just a sour face?" "Did he disobey intentionally or forget?") leads to a blurring of the parental limit.

Putting the announcement in writing adds to its ceremonial nature and thereby to its ability to mark a point of change. Some parents feel uncomfortable because they prefer more natural and spontaneous processes, but the whole point is to establish a limit that deviates from the natural and spontaneous continuum. Setting a limit is like setting a broken leg in a cast. A cast is not natural, but it is necessary to facilitate healing. When the announcement is delivered both verbally and in writing, it contributes to consolidating and setting the selected limit. Parents who do this convey the message, "This is a special occasion because we have reached an intolerable situation!"

Despite the formality, the announcement is not an anonymous or technical event. To the contrary, it indicates an emotional and moral limit because it emphasizes the parents' concern for the child and for the whole family, such as

> "We are going to absolutely resist your disappearing at night because we will not give up on you!"
>
> or
>
> "We will not allow the computer to be on at night because we will not accept your giving up school to get lost in the virtual world."

The announcement ends with a statement that clarifies that the decision arises from the parents' concern for their child. For instance:

> "The present measure arises from our supreme duty and love for you!"
>
> or

"We are doing this because we care about you and we believe in you and in your ability to get over this!"

The announcement is always stated in the first-person plural ("we") rather than in the imperative and in the second person. Do ***not*** use sentences such as

"You must stop hitting your siblings!"

or

"You will not go out at night anymore without permission!"

The reason is twofold:

a. The language of prohibition invites the child to prove the parents are not achieving their goal, and

b. The second-person prohibition neutralizes the parents' human and emotional presence. Commands sound anonymous. That is exactly what we are trying to avoid.

The announcement is not a contract. The child it is not required to agree to it. It is a unilateral message in which the parents announce a change in themselves and in their position. Sometimes, parents say "but she'll never agree!" This comment shows just how far the parents have drifted in their attitude toward their child: They think that any position they take is meaningless unless the child agrees to it. The announcement signifies a substantial change that stops this drifting. Even if the child protests, resists or ignores it or even if they crumple up the page, shred it into pieces, and throw it away, the announcement is not canceled. To the contrary, the child's provocative reaction gives parents an opportunity to say, "You're not expected to agree. We are telling you what *we* are going to do! We gave you a copy of our announcement to be fair to you so that we wouldn't be acting behind your back. We are going to do what we said because it is our duty."

Many parents feel they are unable to make an announcement. They fear the child will react with rejection, rage or derision. These parents got used to not being allowed to insist on any demand to which the child has not agreed. Statements that convey an uncompromising parental duty feel like the violation of unwritten rules. Therefore, many parents feel the need to sweeten their statement with justifications, explanations, and apologies. When they set out to demand something from their child, they quickly go from demand to request, apologies, and complicated explanations.

Eddie, 13, was adopted when he was six. Despite his good relationship with his parents and despite their efforts, they did not feel secure about Eddie's sense of belonging to the family unit. They expressed that feeling starkly: "We adopted him as our son fully, but we're not sure he adopted us!"

Eddie stoked their insecurity when during arguments he would say, "You're not my real parents! You don't love me like real parents!"

Recently, Eddie developed some concerning habits. He began locking himself in his room for long hours and refusing to answer when his parents knocked on the door. He ignored them when they called him to meals and sometimes did not come at all. He was addicted to the computer and responded aggressively when his parents dared interrupt him. He almost completely stopped doing his modest chores, such as walking the dog or taking out the garbage. His parents tried to punish him by reducing his allowance, but Eddie reacted so strongly that they reneged.

Eddie's parents came for counseling and were asked to write an announcement. The text they prepared revealed their parental insecurity:

Dear Eddie,

We love your living with us, and we care about you deeply. We see you as part of the family. But that does not exempt you from helping with the things we ask you for, specifically:

a. We ask you not to lock your door (we don't lock ours either).

b. We appreciate your help taking care of the dog and taking out the garbage. But recently you forget to do it, and we'd like to remind you that those things need to be done.

c. We want to help you not to stay on the computer all the time during summer vacation without doing anything else. We'll ask you to decide what you want to do and do it faithfully.

d. We want you to put down all your other activities when we call you to dinner. It is very important to all of us and also nicer.

We demand that you fulfill all of these requests. This will make the atmosphere at home nicer. These are not hard things to do, and we think it would be good for you.

We love you very much,
Daddy and Mommy

The announcement seeks to put an end to this kind of apologetic stance. Instead it should express a clear stand against drifting, a message in which parents say simply and wholeheartedly: "Here we stand!" and "This is our duty!"

With the help of their counselor the parents reformulated their announcement as a simple statement of their position, without a trace of apology or begging. In the weeks following the delivery of the announcement, the parents dared to insist the door not be locked and that Eddie join them for family meals.

The change in their position was evident when Eddie repeated his claim that they were not his real parents. To this, his father answered simply: "We know that we are your parents because our love and devotion to you are the clearest thing in our lives. We are not going to try to prove to you what is absolutely clear. Whether you are convinced or not, that's up to you!" In this way the parents turned the tables on the question of their parenthood. They stopped explaining, convincing and proving—and Eddie stopped bringing it up.

The Sit-in

Originally, we developed the rite of the sit-in as a tool of resolute resistance by parents against children's acts of violence and self-destruction. In several countries where our approach became famous, the sit-in became its main hallmark. The reason is simple. The sit-in portrays a tangible picture of parental firmness against a drifting toward problem behaviors.

The parents enter the child's room at a quiet time (a sit-in should not be held in the middle of a fight or right after the problem behavior), sit down, and state in simple words the reason for the sit-in. They might say, for instance, "We are not going to allow you to hit your sister. We are going to sit here and wait for a solution so it doesn't happen again!"

After this opening they sit quietly and wait for the child to make a suggestion. Staying silent serves to prevent escalation into argument. This silence does not express disconnection but rather listening. The parents sit silently while conveying attentiveness and openness toward whatever idea the child brings up. The wait can last as much as an hour.

If the child brings up any idea, the parents ask clarification questions in a respectful tone. But if the child's suggestions are unacceptable, such as "I'll stop doing it if you buy me a new computer," or "She started! You always blame me!" the parents reply: "Right now we're looking for a positive solution. If you have any practical suggestion, we will be happy to hear it!"

And they continue sitting silently. Any suggestion, however partial, should be positively received, such as: "It is a step in the right direction. We'll give it a chance and see how things go!" With this statement the sit-in ends.

If the child does not suggest any solution or acts defiantly (cursing or demonstratively ignoring the request), the parents continue sitting quietly without reacting to provocations. Refraining from reacting does not show weakness but self-control. The parents are the ones who initiate and manage the sit-in. If they react to the child's defiance and get into a confrontation, they will be baited and lose the initiative.

If the child demonstratively ignores them and, for example, starts playing with the computer, the parents should not turn it off. This could lead to a serious escalation including a violent outburst. It is better for the parents to continue sitting quietly in the room. They can move their chairs and sit behind the child, although at a safe distance to prevent the child from attacking them for invading their physical space. (Parents can neutralize the computer before the sit-in by taking away the mouse).

If during the sit-in the child does not make any suggestion, the parents leave the room an hour later, saying: "We haven't found a solution yet! We're going to keep looking!" The parents do not punish the child for any sort of behavior during the sit-in. By merely sitting in silent determination, parents reassert themselves as parents after a period of surrender, disregard. or being baited into conflicts. The sit-in concretely symbolizes parental anchoring. It also conveys the message, "We are here, and we are staying here!"

Like the announcement, the sit-in is a ceremony that primarily aims to make a change in the parents. The suggestion the child makes (or doesn't make) is not the critical factor. In many cases, children make a suggestion, but their behavior does not change; whereas in other cases they make no suggestions. but their behavior improves. The critical element in changing the situation is the parents' determined sitting.

Preparation

Parents already begin to change during the preparation stage for the sit-in. Instead of shooting from the hip in the heat of events, parents plan the sit-in, make time for it, coordinate their positions, look for solutions to logistical problems (for instance, having the grandmother come over to watch the other children during the sit-in), and plan how to withstand the child's reactions. Sometimes, parents decide not to hold the sit-in on the same day as the event but on the next day or even later. This does not detract from the effectiveness of the sit-in. Rather, this can make it more effective because the parents demonstrate that they remember and that things are not wiped off the agenda.

The best way for parents to prepare is together. They must think about how to respond to each provocative reaction by the child without being drawn into a problematic reaction. If it is impossible to discuss this with the other parent (for instance, in the case of a single parent or divorced parents who do not communicate), the preparation conversation can be done with another person.

During the preparation conversation, you raise the question, "What could cause the sit-in to deteriorate into a futile argument or make it fall apart?" Merely raising the potential problem scenarios improves the parents' resolve. Their mission is to control themselves as best as they can without being drawn into provocations or preaching, threats, or arguments. Parents must be patient, willing to tolerate discomfort, and willing to listen. This preparation is a kind of crash course because the same patterns that could lead the sit-in to deteriorate also harm other interactions between the parents and child. Therefore, the sit-in is important training for parents' behavior in routine situations as well.

Connected Silence

Even though the sit-in was originally developed for particularly difficult cases, over the years we have discovered its value for parents at-large as well, whose children do not suffer from especially severe behavior patterns. Its special value in these cases is that it offers a special kind of contact. Parents who have learned about our approach from our lectures at schools have told us that by using sit-ins they managed to talk to their children in better ways than before. At first, this surprised us. After all, the instructions for a sit-in are to sit silently and wait for the child to make a proposal. So, how could the sit-in lead to productive conversations? The preparation for sitting silently, it turns out, enabled parents to avoid preaching and scolding, which prevent meaningful contact. Gradually we understood that the parents who make the best use of the sit-in are the ones who, in addition to determination, convey openness and attentiveness. These parents sit silently, in a positive and inviting way. When we focused on the way these parents acted, we learned how to instruct other parents to conduct more effective sit-ins. They should not only say, "we are going to sit here and wait for a solution to make sure the problem behavior does not happen again" but also should add, "anything you tell us about this is important. We will listen and think about it!" After this statement, the silence begins, but it has a unique character. It is a silence of connection. Even if the child behaves defiantly during the sit-in, the parents can say at the end, "we are interested in hearing anything you want to say to us. If you think about anything that you want us to know, we'll be glad to hear it!"

Other Versions of the Sit-In

The contribution of parents at large (which is to say, parents whom we did not counsel, but who implemented the sit-in as they understood it), emanated as well from the invention of original versions, such as the "sit-in on wheels," described in the following case:

> *Gil, the father of Job (11), found out that Job had taken $20 out of Gil's wallet. Job was a restless child but previously had not done anything to worry his parents.*
>
> *First, the parents tried to understand what had prompted Job to steal. They encouraged him to talk, using a sensitive approach, but Job evaded them.*
>
> *Gil's feeling was that Job had gotten into trouble because of a new friend, who had a reputation of being a hooligan. Job's silence may have been meant to protect his friend, who may have induced him to steal.*
>
> *Gil learned about the sit-in from a lecture he heard at school but thought he was not capable of sitting quietly for an entire hour in his son's room. When he told us what he had done instead of the "standard" sit-in, he explained, 'I think I'm just as restless as my son. How could I sit still for a whole hour?'*
>
> *Gil's solution came from his own liking to take long drives. Just driving quietly gave him a feeling of freedom and rest. So, he took Job with him in the car on an early Saturday morning and told him they both needed to think about what had happened. They drove for two hours in almost complete silence. When Job asked him where they were going, Gil answered "It doesn't matter! What matters is that we'll be together and think together!"*
>
> *Two hours later, they stopped at a roadside restaurant. Gil ordered food and drink for both of them and waited quietly for it to be served. Then, he asked Job, "Do you have everything you need?"*
>
> *Job nodded his head. Gil went on: "Is there anything you need and that you might be embarrassed to ask for?"*
>
> *Job shook his head, with tears in his eyes. Gil said to him: "I don't think it was your idea to take the money. I know you, and that's not like you! You don't have to tell me how you got the idea, maybe*

you want to be loyal to a friend. Maybe I'm wrong, but I think you might have been tempted to do something that is not like you and does not become you. Your mom and I are going to keep an eye on you and make sure this doesn't happen again. But I think you will regain our trust."

When they left the restaurant, Gil embraced his son warmly, and Job embraced him back. It was clear that the relationship had gotten stronger and on a more mature and honest basis.

The sit-in can convey both determination and intimacy. Sometimes, the determination element is dominant, sometimes the intimacy. In the case of the "sit-in on wheels." both elements were equally prominent. Gil's quiet drive with Job conveyed determination, whereas sitting in the restaurant conveyed intimacy.

In all of the cases, the sit-in signals the end of disconnection whether the disconnection was caused by helplessness or by anger and escalation. The persistence, self-control, openness, and attentiveness create new circumstances, which places parents' parenthood on a better basis. Therefore, the sit-in serves as a rite of passage from drifting away to parental presence.

Stop Providing the Child with Harmful Things and Conditions

A crucial kind of limit, albeit sometimes difficult to implement, is the limit parents need to set for themselves when they understand that their giving things to a child is itself harmful. We all know situations in which giving is manifestly destructive, like showering a diabetic child with candy or giving a car to a teenager who drives recklessly. These are cases where the parents give children the instrument with which they harm themselves.

The more common cases are those in which the damaging potential is less clear, or alternatively, when the giving is socially acceptable. Look at the examples given here.

a. a personal computer and cell phone are acceptable and even necessary for our children, but children sometimes get addicted to screens, neglect their obligations, or deprive themselves of sleep.

b. Privacy in their bedroom is important to adolescents' development, but teenagers sometimes turn their room into a "parent-free zone," where they can engage in problematic activities unhindered.

c. Money children receive from their parents sometimes serves for gambling, addictive games, or the purchase of hazardous substances.

In the process of setting a limit, parents primarily set a limit for themselves. To do this, they must overcome the confusion and ambiguity that undermine their parenthood.

The trap of normativeness is a common problem undermining the sense of parental legitimacy. Possession of computers cell phones, and spending money as well as children's right to use their room however they want are norms and even taken for granted in our society. Even when the child abuses these things, parents tend to ask themselves, "Am I allowed to stop supplying them?" "Is it legitimate?" "Will it not make my child different?" These doubts seriously undermine parents' resolve. Setting limits on these subjects is difficult enough to do, but it is all the more difficult if the parents have doubts about the legitimacy of doing so. In this situation, parents are particularly vulnerable to criticism from friends, neighbors and other parents; vocal protests by their children; or their internal doubts.

To create the necessary mindset, parents must ask themselves frankly and honestly, "Is the service I provide my child with actually harmful?" Sometimes, it is hard for parents to ask this question, among other reasons because the problematic giving is so taken for granted that it is not even perceived as a privilege conferred by the parent. For many parents, providing a computer, paying the cell phone bill, allowing full privacy in the bedroom, and even giving a generous allowance are like providing food. Even when children become addicted to their computer, use their cell phone for forbidden contacts, seclude themselves in their room day and night, and buy drugs with their allowance, it is hard for the parents to ask themselves whether they might be destroying their child by giving them these things.

The same goes for the support parents continue to provide when the child is already an adult. Parents of grown-up children who are not in school, do not work, and do not show a willingness to function independently sometimes continue providing all of the household services and even add in a car, gas, insurance, and repairs. Sometimes, parents also pay the mounting fines their children accumulate.

The fear of being perceived as bad parents is another trap that stops parents from reaching the obvious conclusion that they are providing their child with support that is destructive. Sometimes, parents justify continuing to give to their child by saying the child is suffering and these things mitigate the child's suffering. However, "consolation giving" is a particularly problematic kind of gifting. When parents decide to compensate for their children's misery, the children receive confirmation that they are indeed miserable. This, then, turns the parents into a link in the vicious circle that deepens children's feeling that they are incompetent and worthless. Another negative consequence is that children learn to see themselves as entitled to all these privileges and gifts. Many parents discover that when they do try to stop destructive gifting, the child cries bitterly that their fundamental rights have been violated.

Parents tend to think that if their children are capable of obtaining in other ways the privileges, they wish to stop bestowing, then any limit is meaningless. This conviction is reflected in statements such as, "There's no point preventing them from using the computer at home since they will just use it at friends'!" Or, "It doesn't help that we tell him he can't do it; he does it, anyway!" The assumption behind these statements is that setting a limit is meaningful only if it manages to block the problematic behavior. Thus, if the child is able to obtain the thing the parents decide to withhold in other ways, any limit set by the parents becomes meaningless.

In reality, the meaningfulness of an established limit extends well beyond blocking the problematic behavior. The parental limit marks the difference between the permitted and the forbidden, gives parents a moral position, and creates an accompanying presence even when the child manages to bypass it. There is a world of difference between the feeling that parents are giving up and the feeling that the parents are fighting for their parenthood even when the child violates their values. Children who experience their parents' giving up lose all sense of being accompanied. They may enjoy the sense of freedom, but they also feel abandoned. On the other hand, the experience of a child who comes up against a warm and firm parental limit is the exact opposite. They feel that their parents are close and are not giving up on them.

These insights have a critical impact on the way parents inform the child about withholding the problematic privileges. The parents announce that their decision reflects their duty to stop harmful gifting. They are helped by their supporters to cope with the problem of normativeness and project the legitimacy of their position. They prepare to cope with the child's attempts to bypass their decision. Sometimes, they manage to make it significantly harder for the child to obtain the harmful things. When sometimes the child manages to obtain them, anyway, the parents say, "We have no way to control you and forcefully stop you from getting harmful things, but we will not supply them to you ourselves. This is our duty as loving parents!"

Sometimes, parents ask which services are really necessary. We think the only service that is taken for granted, regardless of the child's behavior, is food. Even the right to live in the parent's household can in certain conditions stop being taken for granted, for example, when an adult child imposes cruel requirements on the members of the household and uses violence to maintain them. That extreme situation is not rare. We have treated hundreds of families where such tyranny is exercised whether by adolescents or adults, and we are sure we have only discovered the tip of the iceberg of a problem that is quickly spreading throughout modern society.

Following are a number of questions that can help parents examine themselves and decide whether their gifting is problematic:

- "Does my child use the computer or cell phone in a harmful way?"
- "Does my child hide out in his or her room in a concerning way?"
- "Does my child use his or her room for illegitimate purposes?"
- "Does my child use his or her allowance for illegitimate purposes?"

- "Does my child deserve the transportation help I provide? Does my child use the car safely?"
- "Do I do things for my child that are inappropriate for the age and the level of functioning expected from a child of that age?"

When parents take a close look at these points, sometimes they conclude that stopping the harmful privileges is not only legitimate but necessary. This does not make them bad parents. To the contrary, it restores the real basis of their parenthood, which is concern for the child and the rest of the family.

After he was diagnosed with Crohn's disease, Jerry, 16, drastically changed his behavior. He stopped going to school and spent his time with a group of school dropouts. He got up at noon and stayed out till late at night. His parents knew he smoked grass regularly, and sometimes he came home drunk. Once his friends brought him to the hospital in an alcoholic coma.

Jerry got a high allowance, which was normal in their circles. He only wore brand names. He always had the latest model cell phone. His parents, Darren and Vicki, felt helpless when they sought counseling. They were afraid of doing something that would make Jerry angry, make him appear different to his friends, or make him depressed. They were also afraid that if they stopped giving him money, he would ask relatives for money or steal it.

Gradually, the parents managed to develop a plan to recover their presence. They used the extended family, their friends, and community leaders. They realized that their gifting was part of the problem.

One morning, they went into his room and told him, "We realized we are damaging you by giving you money, a cell phone, and the conditions to maintain a destructive lifestyle. We decided to stop your allowance. We are stopping paying for your cell phone. We are stopping buying you brand names. We will not provide you with the conditions for protected and destructive privacy. We will not let you lock yourself in your room. We will continue to supervise you and do everything to improve our relationship with you except for buying your love!"

The parents told the extended family about their plan and asked everyone not to give Jerry money. Darren asked Jerry's grandfather, who was an important figure in Jerry's life, to come over the next day to wake Jerry up in the morning. Two days later Jerry discovered his cell phone account had been turned off. At first, he used savings from the money and gifts he had previously received from his parents and other relatives to pay the cell phone bill, but within a month he had used up all of his money. Once, he stole cash from his mother's wallet, but from that moment on his parents guarded their money carefully. They also took the valuables out of the house out of fear that Jerry would try to sell them.

When Jerry invited his friends over and secluded himself with them in his room, his mother knocked on his door. Jerry refused to answer. She then called Darren, and they both said through the door that under these circumstances, his friends needed to leave. After a few minutes of discussion, the friends got up and left the house.

Jerry managed to find a few temporary jobs to pay for his pastimes. Three months later, he joined a community program for school dropouts. Gradually, some of his rights were restored. However, additional improvements came slowly. In retrospect, his parents concluded that only two years later, Jerry began to settle into a positive routine. They had no doubt that stopping their uncontrolled giving was a key component in his rescue.

Making Amends

Even little children understand the meaning of acts meant to make up for hurting another person. In my book, *The New Authority: Family, School, and Community,* I described a program to a group of kindergartens, where children from the age of four were asked by their teachers and parents to make amends when they hurt other children. The children understood the meaning of the request and the need for amends. A board was hung on the main wall of the complex presenting the token gifts that had been given as amends to children who had been hurt. The use of amends became an important part of the kindergartens' fight against violence against both children and teachers. It affected both the children and the adults. It led to greater involvement of parents and improved the alliance between the parents and teachers. The atmosphere in the kindergarten improved, and violence dropped sharply.

Amends are a key element of relations between people in all societies and at all ages. It is hard to overstate their value in educating children. When parents explain to their children the need to make up for harming another, they achieve an array of goals:

- They develop the child's sensitivity to the suffering of others.
- They improve the child's sense of responsibility.
- They contribute to repairing the child's relationship with the community.
- The children restore a positive internal sense that even though they hurt someone they can feel like a good person again.
- They create an event that will be etched in memory and help distinguish between the way things were and the way they are going to be.

The first stage of the process is to have a conversation in which the parents raise the need to make an amend. The parents must have the conversation under conditions conducive to positive communication. There is no contradiction between the requirement for amends and pleasant circumstances of the amends conversation, such as sitting at a café. Requiring amends is different from traditional punishment. Therefore, there is no concern that by creating pleasant conditions the child will be "receiving a prize for a bad action."

The conversation should begin with the simple statement: "You hurt X. We want to think together how you can make up for that." The harm should be described in simple and concrete language. Words such as "you hit," "you stole," "you ruined," or "you cursed" serve to clarify the harm. The offended party might be a child, a teacher, the cleaning lady, the class, or the school. Often the child will raise defensive arguments. It is important to listen to these arguments and treat them seriously, such as, "We understand you didn't do it for no reason; you did it because you were frustrated. But you hurt someone, and that is not allowed even if they made you angry first." Sometimes, the child will deny the transgression, despite clear evidence of it. It is important to counter a false claim directly but nonconfrontationally, such as, "This is not about proof but simply about repairing the situation, and we are willing to help you do it."

For some children this will not be enough and they will continue to claim they are being falsely accused. In this case, the discussion must be stopped even if the child is frustrated. The parents can say, "The situation gets both you and us into trouble because we are your parents. We are part of this because you are our child and we are responsible for you. We have to look for a solution that repairs the situation both for you and for ourselves." The parents thereby create a new situation: They are part of the damage and part of the amends.

Indeed, it is both socially and legally normative for parents to bear some of the responsibility when their child hurts someone. Children can understand when their parents explain: "When you hurt someone, we are also part of it. For instance, if you do damage, we have to pay." In addition, the parents experience (or ought to experience) shame for their child hurting someone. Their social status can suffer, especially if they do not react properly. Therefore, the statement "we are part of this" is both a normative message and consistent with reality.

When parents take part in the action it makes it easier for the child to make amends without feeling humiliated. When the parents say to the child, "we will go to the teacher together, give her a letter signed by all three of us, and support you in the preparation and in the execution of making amends," they provide their child with broad shoulders. The child makes the amends as part of a family that provides him or her with support and encouragement. These conditions allow the child to "make amends while standing tall."

Children understand this well. The message is even stronger when the people around them respond in kind. For instance, the teacher can tell a child who hurt someone, "We care about your pride. So, we are asking your parents to do it with you and help you make amends." After the child has made amends, the teacher can say, "Good job! You and your parents are a great family!" Even children who at first protested the amends feel pride when the teacher includes them and their family in praise for the action they took.

The fact that the parents share responsibility for the amends allows them to act even when the child refuses. Thus, if the child hurt a classmate but refuses to apologize, the parents can bring the teacher an apology letter from them and the child. If the child damaged property, the parents can bring in addition to the letter a substitute item or monetary compensation. In these cases, they tell their child, "we are responsible with you! So, we are apologizing and making amends because it is our duty. You can join with us in making amends, but if you choose not to, we will decide how to charge you for the compensation."

It is important to say this in a factual tone of voice. Any threatening tone reinforces the child's tendency to resist. The parent's message is even stronger if a supporter who is close to the child tells the child, "I know your parents are writing an apology letter and compensating for the harm you did. It is their duty both to you and to the others. I'm willing to help you join in making amends as part of the family so that you feel you're doing it in a dignified way."

If the child still refuses, the parents can make the amends and then inform the child how much is owed. There are different ways to charge the child, such as deducting part or all of any allowance the child is receiving for a certain period of time (which means the child pays in installments), deducting the fair share from the child's savings, or deducting services that cost money. The important point, however, is not that the child pay back the exact value of the damage. Amends are symbolic of the process of repairing a broken bond. Therefore, any contribution, even an unwilling one, can be meaningful.

A simple statement is the best way to give the message a chance to reverberate in the child's mind. In some cases, we have seen a child who initially refused to cooperate with the familial amends indicate that the parents' making amends did make an impression. This makes the making of amends essentially different from traditional punishments.

Amends and compensation can occur within the family as well, such as when a child hurts a sibling, parents, or family property. The father can tell the child, "You hurt your mother. You must make amends for the harm. If you want to think with me how to compensate her, I will support you and help you." If the child refuses, the father can say, "If you aren't ready, I will make the compensation myself and then think about how you can pay your share of the cost."

An especially good compensation inside the family is an outing with the offended party. Thus, the father can take the offended mother or sister to a movie or café. The offending child will share the costs in a way the parents decide upon.

An important element in making amends is showing a personal example. Parents show personal example when they take responsibility and participate in the process of making amends. They give a powerful example when they are willing to make amends for their own actions. Several parents we worked with told us about cases where they felt they had misbehaved, such as screaming at their child. Their willingness to admit the mistake, express regret, and honestly state their intention to do what they could to avoid repeating the behavior became in some cases a turning point in their relationships. For many parents, it is hard to admit a mistake so long as they feel helpless, but when they become stronger, they gain the courage to do so.

Making amends is a particularly profound illustration of the loving limit. Unlike a traditional punishment, which is imposed on the child from the outside and in which the parent merely functions as the "executor" of the painful outcome, in making amends the parents are fully involved. They stand with the child, they share the responsibility, they take on themselves at least part of the burden, they help the child perform the act, and they help protect the child's dignity. Therefore, the selection and enactment of a specific compensation gives the child a sense of belonging. When the child is told, "You and your parents did a wonderful thing!" the child experiences satisfaction and belonging. It is very rare for a child to react by saying, "They went against my wishes!" Usually the child is happy to receive the praise for themselves and their family. Even if the child does not immediately relate to the act of making amends, it gradually sinks in, partly because it contributes to improving relations with the people surrounding the child. Usually, after having made amends, the child's aggressive actions diminish even if the child has refused to cooperate—as if the child were embarrassed to be violent after amends having been made on his or her behalf.

Summary

Through the loving limit, a parent sends the message, "Here I stand!" This message expresses their values, and their attitude. The process of setting a loving limit begins with a self-examination by parents, in which red lines are determined. Optimally, this process includes both parents as well as additional significant people in their sphere. In this way the parental limit expresses not only the parents themselves but is morally validated by a broader context. The loving limit expresses the parental standing over time. It is not a momentary process but rather a decision, announcement, execution, and follow-up. It is a limit with a past, present, and future. The child experiences not only prohibition and sanction but ongoing presence. With a loving limit, parents systematically avoid any attempt to subdue, control, or dictate. They identify "ping-pong" interactions that perpetuate the conflict with the child and stand firm against provocations without being drawn into them. Instead of futile attempts to convince the child to stop making problematic use of the support they provide, the parent stops giving these things as their supreme duty. Instead of multiple problematic sanctions, parents seek to include the child in making amends. By doing this, parents provide a personal example, recruit support and legitimacy, and turn the response to the problematic behavior into a moral response. Even if the child does not instantly accept the amend-making process and the actual amends, the concept gradually seeps into their heart.

Review and Application

- Whenever you set a limit for your child, set a limit for yourself first. This limit is the red line that you are determined to defend.
- Try to identify your reactions that contribute to a continuing power struggle. Arguments, long explanations, preaching, and repeated scolding only fan the flames.
- Notice your tendency toward "no-chatter." The vaccination against it is to produce "no-anchors."
- Learn how to talk in the first-person plural ("we"). Avoid statements in the language of "you have to!"
- Check whether there are things you give to your child that the child uses destructively.

- It is essential to stop providing the child with devices that can be used destructively even if the child can obtain the same things elsewhere.
- Ask yourself if you are giving your child "consolation prizes" that reinforce the child's self-conception as miserable.
- Ask yourself whether you have reacted to your child inappropriately in the past. Consider the possibility of apologizing in a dignified way. It will not weaken you but, rather, strengthen your child's image of you.
- Offer to help your child make amends. Say that you are one family and therefore you must make amends together.
- Include a supporter to explain to the child the need for making amends.
- If the child does not cooperate, make the amends on behalf of the child and think about how to charge the child later.

Chapter Six

Fears

Fears do not exist only in the child's head but also in the space between the child and parents. The reason is simple: a fearful child instinctively turns to parents for help. That is an innate reaction rooted in the survival instinct. The tendency to cling to the nearest strong adult who can provide protection and security is universal. Indeed, parents are the guarantee that children can grow up safe and sound despite their weakness and vulnerability.

However, the instinct to take refuge with the parent does not always make the distinction between real and imaginary dangers. The child runs to a parent for protection even when there is no real danger. What can the parent do in such situations? How can the parent help the child both calm down and grow up?

Support, Not Protection

The principle of giving the child support rather than protection paves the way to overcoming fears. Little babies need a heaping dose of parental protection and support, of course. In the first months of life, the mother is virtually attached to the baby. She feeds it, embraces it, and soothes it. Today, unlike in past generations, fathers also play an important role in the lives of their infants. The mother and father alternate and complete each other to create the infant's first interpersonal experiences, such as through mutual gazes, increased imitation of the baby's facial expressions, and physical and vocal games. That said, from the earliest months of life the baby benefits from the parents' letting it be alone at certain times in order to develop the initial foundations for self-soothing and independent action.

Sleep Problems

In the first chapter, we mentioned some research findings about babies with sleeping problems. Paradoxically, these babies actually need their parents to be able to withstand their crying without immediately rushing in to soothe them. If the parents immediately rush to embrace and soothe them, the babies' sleep problems are not resolved. Rather, infants who cannot sleep without their parents being attached to them experience a kind of separation anxiety. Their behavior is very similar to that of older children who suffer from such anxiety. Children with separation anxiety cry and cling to their parents to prevent their parents from leaving them even for a moment. Separation anxiety, like sleep problems, tends to continue or even worsen when the parents always respond to distress calls. On the other hand, when parents show the infant that they are around but without creating actual physical contact, the problem gradually abates. These parents support their children rather than protecting them.

The research on children with sleep problems raised another finding: When parents always respond to their infants' cries of distress, it is not only harder for the infants to fall asleep by themselves, but also their sleep is less sound. They wake up more frequently, stay awake longer, and toss and turn more during the night. On the other hand, when parents learn to wait a few minutes before approaching and soothing their babies without taking them out of the crib, babies not only learn how to fall asleep more easily, they also sleep more soundly. When they wake up in the middle of the night, they can stay calm for a few moments before falling back to sleep. This shows that parents' ability to resist the urge to immediately rush to rescue their baby from its distress makes the baby calmer! We think the explanation is that the baby learns the critical skill of self-soothing.

Protectiveness against Distress

Protective parents try to prevent their children from feeling any distress. When children show signs of anxiety, parents rush to soothe them or to remove the scary stimulant immediately. Protective parents give the impression that they are afraid of their child experiencing fear. Indeed, these parents tend much more than others to believe that the very experience of anxiety can hurt a child. The truth is very different: Feelings of anxiety are not harmful unless experienced under extreme circumstances, such as war or abuse. On the contrary, children need to experience anxiety in order to learn how to cope with it. Parents' attempt to prevent their children from feeling any anxiety is what actually proves to be harmful.

There are several reasons that parental protectiveness perpetuates anxiety problems:

- Children don't learn they can tolerate anxiety;
- They don't learn that anxiety is limited in time, which means it tends to go down after it goes up;
- They don't develop coping skills but wait for their parent to "rescue" them;
- They get the impression their parents are afraid for them to feel fear;
- They get the message that their parents don't think they can cope; and
- They learn from their parent that it is important to avoid any anxiety-inducing situation.

Each one of these processes undermines the child's development and resilience.

The negative lessons children learn from parents' protectiveness can be summarized by a series of beliefs they develop about themselves and about the states of anxiety they experience:

- Feeling fear is terrible!
- I cannot survive it!
- My parents cannot tolerate my fear!
- If they don't rescue me, my fear will just go up and up!

- I must avoid any situation that might cause me fear!
- If I start to feel fear, I must immediately call for help!

When parents develop the ability to support instead of protect, they allow their child to break free of those damaging beliefs.

There is another parental position that is the opposite of protectiveness, which can also undermine the anxious child's ability to cope. That is the reaction of parents who get angry and demand that the child get over his or her fears right away. These parents tend to believe you must throw the child into the water and let him or her swim. Conversely, the child must be punished or scolded and preached to until the fear stops. We call these parents demanding parents. We can imagine the protective parent carrying their children in their arms and thereby preventing them from learning how to walk; the demanding parent, on the other hand, pushes them until they fall.

Demanding parents, just like protective parents, act out of good intentions, but when the parents' demands outstrip the child's current abilities, the child cannot benefit from trying to meet them. If we imagine the task facing the child as a step the child must climb up, the demanding parent makes the step much higher and steeper. For instance, the demanding parent might try to encourage the anxious child to be brave by giving a personal example ("let me show you there is nothing to be afraid of!"). Admiring the parent's courage, the child feels inferior and incompetent in comparison. Thus, the demanding parent's personal example achieves the opposite result, and the child is convinced of having no chance of fulfilling the parent's expectations.

Now, the parent will be disappointed and conclude that the child isn't trying hard enough or doesn't want to overcome the difficulty. The parent might even interpret the child's behavior as manipulation designed solely to gain treats and an easing of demands. This disappointment can lead the parent to anger, to more absolute demands, and even to giving an ultimatum: "Either you start doing it, or I give up!" And this stance might create a disconnection from their child.

Just as the child learns negative lessons when parents overprotect them, the same happens when the parent is demanding. In this case, the child might develop problematic feelings such as:

- All I do is disappoint them over and over again!
- If I'm afraid, I'm inferior!
- I have no chance of meeting expectations!
- They think I'm lying!
- I have a double reason to be afraid: from the thing itself and from my parents' anger!

Both the overprotective parent and the demanding parent deprive children of a stabilizing experience of anchoring against the fears that unsettle them. Protective parents don't serve as an anchor because they impulsively rush to protect and rescue. Demanding parents don't serve as an anchor because they are irritable, pushy, and short-tempered. Both add to the maelstrom that tugs at the child instead of helping the child to stabilize.

Destabilization is maximized when one parent protects and the other demands. This very common situation occurs because a protective parent tends to make the other parent demanding and vice versa. Thus, faced with a protective spouse, the other parent thinks, "I'm the only one who demands my child function, so I must do it more forcefully!" Whereas faced with a demanding spouse, the other parent tends to think, "I'm the only one who protects my child so I must do it more strongly!" This seesaw between the two parents is a recipe for deepening the child's anxieties.

Do fears go away by themselves?

We all know that little children have more fears than big children. Fear of animals, the dark, monsters, strangers, or being alone, are much more common in the early years. For most children, these fears gradually disappear following natural growth processes. The recognition of these processes will help parents "get out of the way."

Increase of Independent Activity

As children grow up, the range of their independent activity gradually increases. This process is a natural result of the child's physical development. Children learn how to crawl, walk, and run by biological design. Each such stage increases the child's capacity to function independently. Motor skill development enables children to do things for themselves that previously required their parents' help. Not only is the development of those skills biologically programmed, but so are the drive and will to use them.

Little children repeatedly try to master new activities. They enjoy the practice and the control. The expansion of their range of independent action exposes them to new stimulations. Some of these initially spark anxiety, but repeated exposure and skill acquisition make the anxiety go away. For instance, a child who stands for the first time without leaning on something shows signs of fear and caution as if the child is a little worried by his or her independence. The urge to go forward, though, makes the child try again and again. This is an instructive example of overcoming anxiety because every baby without exception manages to do it.

Other examples include developing the ability to crawl away from parents, to be in situations where parents are not in eye contact, to stay with a stranger without the parent's presence, and so on. In each of these cases, most children experience some initial anxiety, but the urge toward independence, the encouragement of the environment, and the very repetition of the attempts, make the anxiety gradually go away.

Being with Other People

As children grow, they spend an increasingly greater amount of time in the company of people outside of their nuclear family. The expansion of their physical space parallels the expansion of their social space. They spend more time with others, first with the parents present and then without them. This process contributes significantly to the natural overcoming of anxiety. For instance, being with other people helps babies overcome stranger anxiety, a common reaction of infants.

Research on infant development finds that between the ages of six months and a year many children demonstrate distress when someone outside of the nuclear family tries to pick them up or stay alone with them in a room. This phenomenon, called "stranger anxiety," was considered universal until anthropological research proved otherwise. It found that in cultures where the norm is for babies to be held and cared for by other people in the first place there is no stranger anxiety. Most probably in these societies the pathological phenomena of social anxiety are less common than in our society. The reason is clear. These children get early experience spending time with others without their parents being present. Being with people outside of the nuclear family helps overcome anxiety not only in babies but also in older children. The reason is twofold:

a. with other people, children are less regressive (e.g., less dependent and babyish) than with their parents; and

b. other people are less inclined to immediately protect the child when the first signs of anxiety appear.

This "insensitivity" promotes adjustment in children. The very fact that the people around them do not rush to protect them against anxiety signals to children that the situation is not as dangerous as perceived. We tend to look around us to get confirmation of our emotions. When other people signal to us there is something to be afraid of, we see this as proof that our fear is justified. However, when others do not, we conclude there is nothing to be afraid of.

More Obligations

As children grow, they need to fulfill more obligations. There is an essential connection between obligations and overcoming anxiety. Obligations are situations in which the child gets the message, "there's no choice, you have to do this!"

A classic example is starting kindergarten. For many children, it is hard to stay alone at kindergarten for the first time, especially if previously they were with their parents all the time. But because education is compulsory by law, parents give them the message "there is no choice!" Even if it is hard for parents bringing their children to kindergarten for the first time, the fact that it is obligatory helps parents overcome their anxiety and leave the child at kindergarten. Some children cry bitterly, but in the vast majority of cases the child gets over it, if not on the first day then in a few days.

This is a significant developmental achievement. Even if the child can't put it into words, the experience of overcoming a fear will be etched in his or her psyche. The child will say, "It was hard, but I did it!" Such moments of pride recur throughout all the years of childhood and adolescence. A school-age child says proudly, "I got over it!" An adolescent says,

"I can't believe how hard it was, but I did it!" Such experiences build our self-image and give us the spine that enables us to meet the challenges we face in life. Expression of appreciation by others, however important, is not enough for us to develop a sense of worth. We also need experiences of overcoming difficulty. Therefore, children who are not required to fulfill any obligations actually suffer from deprivation! The deprivation is not related to love because sometimes parents relieve children of all obligations precisely out of boundless love. Unfortunately, in those cases, children suffer from a deprivation of obligations, or of experiences that say: "There's no choice! You have to do it!" Without such experiences, it is hard for children to develop stamina against anxiety and frustration. Obligations not only build our social identity; they also build our sense of self-worth and competence.

These processes are part of normative development and to some extent exist for every child. Therefore, most children spontaneously overcome their early childhood fears. Sometimes, though, parents inadvertently interfere with that natural process. Some parents feel anxiety when children become "too" independent, which leads them to run after their children to "rescue them from themselves."

Alternatively, parents are either afraid to leave their children in the care of others, or they take them back into their arms when they notice the first signs of discomfort. Inadvertently, these parents increase their children's stranger anxiety and get in the way of the process of their learning to cope with distress.

Most children manage to overcome childhood fears even if their parents sometimes get in the way. However, for children who are naturally anxious and avoidant, this can be problematic. Research shows that children who develop resistant and strong fears, namely children with anxiety disorders, display these tendencies in early childhood, even in infancy. Their nervous systems overreact to threatening stimulants. Many of them are born to parents who also suffer from a tendency toward anxiety. For these children, the combination of their basic sensitivity and a protective or anxious parent leads to the development of an anxiety disorder.

In order for parents to overcome the drive toward overprotection, they need a clear and unequivocal premise to serve them as a fixed point to which they can anchor themselves and stand firm against the drift of the child's fears. Fortunately, research into anxiety provides a clear and proven finding that can serve as such a premise for parents. The finding, substantiated by countless studies, is that avoidance responses deepen and perpetuate anxiety, whereas systematic exposure to the frightening situations is the key to overcoming them.

Avoidance and Exposure

Avoidance is a necessary reaction when it comes to real dangers. Children naturally avoid stimulants that cause physical pain as well as situations of actual danger like high places. In anxiety disorders, by way of contrast, the child develops avoidance reactions to situations that not only are not dangerous but are actually necessary for normal functioning. Thus, children with social anxiety will vigorously avoid situations where they will have to be with other children, children with separation anxiety will avoid separation from their parents even for a moment, and children with fear of sicknesses will avoid any situation where there is even the slightest chance of contagion. Avoidance creates negative circuits that worsen the anxiety and deepen the child's inability to cope.

Just like avoidance is the universal process that perpetuates anxiety disorders, exposure to frightening situations is the universal process that enables overcoming them. Exposure increases the level of anxiety in the immediate term but systematically reduces it if exposure continues. The experience of fear occurs mainly ahead of the encounter with the frightening situation and in its first moments. As time goes by and the disaster the child fears does not materialize, anxiety drops, and coping skills improve. Just like avoidance creates a vicious circle, so does exposure create a virtuous circle. Children discover that the intensity of the anxiety goes down, that they can tolerate it, and that they can do things they previously were too afraid to do.

The best exposure experiences are gradual. The attempt to expose the child all at once to the scary situation can be a trap. In such situations, the child will do anything to escape the situation. Further, the child might be overcome by a sense of helplessness. Many children then develop a deep resistance to any exposure following such a failed attempt at full exposure.

In treating anxiety disorders, the exposure process is gradual, all the while giving the child support. The task the child needs to cope with is divided into small steps, so that each step is not too steep.

On the other hand, parents must not be afraid to expose their child more rapidly to an anxiety-producing situation when a suitable opportunity arises. For instance, when the child wants to participate in an attractive activity that necessitates exposure to scary stimulants. These opportunities open a window to rapid progress. The child then makes a developmental leap, which may be very different from the gradual process by which anxiety is usually conquered.

> *When I was a child, I suffered from serious fears that not only caused me much suffering but also limited my ability to enjoy activities that were very attractive to me. My parents tended not to expose me to difficult situations, especially after an attempt to leave me at their friends' farm failed miserably when I woke up at night crying and begging for my parents to take me home that very night. About two years later, my father took me to visit my brother, who was three years older than me, at summer camp. I spent the whole weekend there with my father, and before we left one of the counselors asked me if I would like to stay. He took me to have dinner with the group that I found the most attractive in the whole camp. Then, he took me to meet my father and told him: "Haim is a real part of the group! Nobody wants him to go home! Would you let him stay?" Only years later did I find out that this scheme was devised together with my father. When my father went home without me, he told my mother, who was very protective, that I had begged to stay (which was true). For me, this was a seminal experience that gave me the strength to confront my grave fears in other situations as well.*

Changing Parents' Attitudes

Overcoming the Fear of the Child Being Afraid

Parents who rush to extract their child from any anxiety-inducing situation signal that they are afraid of their child being afraid. The message they inadvertently send is that fear is something terrible and everything possible should be done to avoid it. This is called an "anxiety alliance." In other words, instead of the parent being the child's ally and demonstrating strength in the face of fear, the parent's anxiety "forges an alliance" with the child's anxiety so that the child feels increased anxiety. In order to let go of the fear of the child being afraid, parents should know that the very experience of anxiety, to the extent that most anxious children experience it, is not in itself harmful. Parents who are characterized by high levels of fear of their child experiencing fear usually have the opposite belief. They believe that anxiety can be traumatic and leave deep scars on the child's psyche, but the vast majority of children's anxieties, even if the subjective experience is serious, are harmless.

What is harmful is avoidance, which systematically undermines normal functioning and development. It is also important to know that anxiety abates after a relatively short time due to simple physiological mechanisms. Anxiety has to do with the activity of the hormonal system (excretion of adrenaline and noradrenalin), an increase in cardiovascular activity (a rise in breath rate, heart rate and blood pressure), and a rise in muscle tension. The purpose of these responses is to prepare the organism for the urgent fight-or-flight survival response. In the absence of an actual existential danger, the body manufactures processes that counter the rise in adrenaline and noradrenalin, cardiovascular activity, and muscle tension. Therefore, anxiety is a mechanism that neutralizes itself naturally. When children are exposed to the anxiety-inducing stimulant and remain in the situation, they discover that after an initial increase their anxiety drops. Children who are willing to undergo cognitive behavioral therapy for anxiety report such responses as, "I thought my anxiety would go up until I would die or go crazy, but I found out that it actually goes down!" Experiences of this kind are critical for the development of resilience.

However, sometimes children are not willing to go through the experience that will teach them that things are not that bad. In this case, a change in the parents' approach might be the basic condition for changing the child's approach as well.

Parents who receive suitable instruction can affect their children's experiences of anxiety even if the child firmly refuses any help for the anxiety problem. This is not a rare phenomenon. Some 50% of children with anxiety disorders refuse treatment. In our study that focused precisely on children who refuse treatment of any kind, we instructed parents how to go from protectiveness to support and thereby gradually expose their children to the anxiety-producing stimulants. After ten weeks of treatment, the children's anxiety levels dropped significantly. Their progress was identical to that of children who were willing to receive treatment for their anxiety problem. To our surprise, after the parents underwent the instruction process, the vast majority of the children changed their minds and were willing to receive treatment for themselves too. When they were asked why they changed their minds, most of them said, "Before I didn't think I could survive if I had to be in a scary situation. Now I have learned that I can survive. So, maybe if I get treatment my fear will go away even more!"

Maintaining a Normal Functioning Framework

The big temptation for parents in the face of their child's anxiety is to decrease their demands for normal functioning in order to reduce the child's suffering. For instance, parents give up the expectation for their children to sleep in their own bed if they have night fears, go everywhere with them if they suffer from separation anxiety, delay or cancel their attendance of preschool if they show distress, let them stay home if they're afraid to go to school, and accommodate the house rules to demands that come from an anxiety disorder. These processes may not end with childhood but continue into adolescence and even adulthood. In their helplessness to face their children's experience of distress, parents sometimes provide them with a "degenerative haven," which is a protective environment that greatly reduces the chances of normal functioning.

A 19-year-old boy suffered from a severe fear of thunder. In his distress, he put incessant pressure on his parents to build him a soundproof room. Finally, his parents acquiesced. Every time a storm threatened, he secluded himself in his room, and even added to the quiet by using a soundproof headset.

This reaction did not help. On the contrary, he began to fear any situation where there was a minimal chance not only of a thunderstorm but also of rain. Gradually, his fears got so bad that he spent most of his time in the safe room. He pressured his parents and grandparents to install a sophisticated video system in it. Gradually, the shelter his parents built him became a degenerative haven, that facilitated his deterioration to his lowest level of functioning ever.

This extreme case illustrates a process that appears in different ways in many young people's lives. The phenomenon of young adults' disengagement from the outside world and their seclusion in the home has become increasingly frequent over the past several decades. In Japan, it has become a veritable epidemic. The phenomenon is called *hikikomori*, and the official estimate is that there are more than one million such young men (the disorder mostly affects males) in Japan, living in complete seclusion from the outside world. In our research, we documented similar phenomena in the Western world and proposed ways to treat them.

The negative consequences of degenerative haven provided by parents are also evident when the problem does not reach the dimensions of "hikikomori." Countless youths forego school, employment, and even social lives due to social anxiety, fear of failure, and performance anxiety. Parents inadvertently support these processes when they supply their children with a degenerative haven, by providing all of their demands of sustenance, unlimited privacy and Internet. Apparently, electronic services severely worsen the tendency to isolate, to the point that it can be asserted that if it weren't for the existence of virtual reality, the frequency of the phenomenon would be immeasurably less. In fact, these young people choose to give up the real world for the virtual world, which is free of the difficulties of the outside world.

To effectively maintain a framework of normal functioning, parents need a clear concept of duty. Nothing symbolizes the current parental erosion and drift better than the outdatedness surrounding the concept of duty. For many people, the word *duty* has assumed a shrill, irritating and archaic sound. The ideal is for children to act not out of a sense of duty but only out of understanding and consent. According to this concept, when a child refuses to carry out an obligation, the only legitimate solution is dialogue and persuasion. Indeed, dialogue and persuasion are key processes in child rearing. Parents do have to explain to children why certain things are necessary. But what should they do when the child is not convinced? Or when they refuse to have a dialogue? Or when they drag the discussion on forever? The belief that dialogue and persuasion are the only legitimate bases for motivating children leads parents into total helplessness in the face of the child's refusal.

Sometimes, parents choose the option of therapy, as a sort of very long extension of the process of dialogue and persuasion. They hope that at the end of the process the child will really be persuaded from within. The truth is that no human society has ever managed to survive without clear duties that apply to those who do not consent to them as well.

In our society, too, where the value of dialogue is very high, there are situations in which the dialogue must stop and be replaced by duty. Indeed, the absolute reliance on dialogue can create endless processes. We all know children who mire their elders in endless discussions. These children are well aware that as long as the discussion continues action is put on hold. Parents treat their children's impressive capacity of argumentation with a mixture of helplessness and respect. Almost every parent who tells us how their child is able to keep a discussion going forever accompanies their description with a smile of appreciation. Indeed, the appreciation is deserved, but the helplessness is harmful. Parents should be capable of stopping the discussion, even in the absence of consent. Where every discussion should end is duty. This is true even when the child refuses to accept it. In these cases, parents must become the determined representatives of duty. The message that ends the discussion is, "This is our duty!" With this, parents signal that the child's duty is their duty, too. When the parents end the discussion by asserting their duty, the focus moves from words to action. Parents give the message that from here on they will act according to their duty, regardless of the child's consent. The statement, "It is our duty!" also conveys the ultimate message of parental care: "Here we stand. We have no choice!"

Parental duty is the guarantee that the parents will take decisive action to maintain the child's normal functioning. It is the fulcrum of the parental lever that will enable the child to overcome his or her fears. Relying on their duty enables parents to stop problematic situations like their child's continuing to sleep in their bed, their child's refusal to part from them even for a moment, school avoidance, and more.

Parents explain the change with the simple phrase, "This is our duty!" But that is not the end of the parents' job. Now, they must act to set a loving and personal limit to the child's problem behavior. In so doing, they must not feel that they are doing something unkind to their child. This doesn't make them "bad parents," rather, the opposite. Only by standing firm can they provide their children with the anchor that will help them get over the anxiety that is making them drift away.

Moyshele, 9, was the youngest son of an ultra-Orthodox family. He was the first son in the family, born six years after the youngest of his seven sisters. His parents, Menachem and Leah, and his sisters, treated him with kid gloves.

Moyshele was fastidious, with acute sensory sensitivity, which was expressed by prominent expressions of impatience if a piece of clothing didn't come out of the laundry soft enough, if his toast was a little burned, or if the seam of his sock pressed his foot. His separation anxiety forced his mother or one of his sisters to stay with him at all times. When his mother couldn't stay with him, one of his sisters had to miss school or take a day off from work to take care of him.

In the last two years, Moyshele had missed a lot of school. It happened every time he woke up with a bad physical sensation, after an unpleasant encounter with one of his teachers, or when he woke up from a bad dream. On days like that, the whole family organized to provide him with constant companionship. No one in the family dared to protest being absolutely chained to Moyshele's needs.

His parents came to consulting after Moyshele had missed an entire month of school. After a meeting with the parents and a second meeting with his sisters and brothers-in-law, the therapist gave the family the following message, "I don't think Moyshele has any mental disorder. The biggest problem in his life is that he has the status of a prince who is above all duty. Not only above his own duties, but also above everybody else's duties as well. If he so wills, his parents' and his sisters' place his desires about their own duties. They cancel a day of school or work because Moyshele needs it. As long as he has the status of the bender of duties, he will not be able to grow. He is still far from taking any duties upon himself. In order for that to happen, he first needs to get the feeling that others have duties that cannot be forsaken."

This formulation led for the first time to grumblings of protest over Moyshele's unshakable princehood, first among his sisters and then from his mother as well. Practically speaking, a "rotation of duties" was established. This rotation did not refer to the duty of taking care of Moyshele, but rather to the duty of the caretakers to go back to their own duties (school or work) as soon as they were called upon to do so.

When the program began, it was decided that whoever came to watch Moyshele received a "duty call," namely a phone call demanding their immediate return to school or work. The brothers-in-law happily filled the role of the duty callers, among other reasons because they were sick and tired of their wives being subject to the whims of the "prince." When a duty call came in, Moyshele could decide (on the spot) whether he wanted to stay home alone or go with the sister in charge to school or to her work.

It was not very comfortable to spend time at those places. At the younger sisters' school, he would have to stay with the guard at the gate. The guard was a no-nonsense man who did not recognize princely rights. At his sisters' or his mother's work, Moyshele had to stay in another room so as not to get in the way.

Within a few days, his father took him back to school. Counseling went on for a few more weeks to guarantee that Moyshele didn't go back to the status of the duty-bending prince.

Over the years, there were a few more situations in which the family came back to counseling, to reassert some of the duties that may have eroded. When he was 14, Moyshele moved without any particular difficulty to a residential school, as was the custom in his community.

Getting Out of Isolation

Parents ask why they need the support of others to help their children deal with their anxieties. Can't they do it alone? As we explained in the chapter about support, Parents' efficiency increases for many reasons when they are helped by a network of supporters. We must remember that anxious children and their parents are so accustomed to each other's conduct surrounding the anxiety that they always act the same way, like a well-oiled machine. The child knows exactly how to pressure the parents, and parents react almost automatically to the child's distress signals. Under these circumstances, the entrance of others brings fresh air into the system. Now, there is wiggle room that didn't exist before. In the perfectly-attuned cogwheel of parent and child, the entry of supporters creates a space for new movements. Further, while the child tends to be particularly anxious, dependent, and babyish in the presence of the parent, in the presence of others, the child displays a more mature and functional personality. The involvement of others also validates expectations of normative functioning. These processes create a completely new mental and interpersonal environment. If previously the anxiety had an ideal environment in which to thrive, now the anxiety is in an environment that encourages coping.

In our work with families with children who have anxiety disorders, we have seen numerous situations in which the involvement of supporters creates a change in the child's and parents' ability to cope with anxiety situations. A noteworthy example is in the case of separation anxiety. When relatives, friends, or nursery school staff receive instructions on how to deal with children exhibiting separation anxiety, children cope better. Another example is of children with Obsessive-Compulsive Disorder (OCD), namely, children with an extreme fear of contamination or the need to perform senseless actions with ritualistic repetition to relieve their anxieties. These children cope much better with problematic situations when they are with others.

Yet another example, concerning a much more common fear, is a process we developed to help families in which the child refuses to sleep in his or her own bed and sleeps in the parents' bed every night: The parents are instructed to plan a long weekend in which they spend at least two nights away from home. Supporters close to the child and the family (such as aunts, uncles, or close friends) babysit the child. These supporters are instructed how to respond to the child's distress calls. They tell the child that he or she is allowed to call them every ten minutes and that they will come into the room and spend a short time there. They tell the child they will not take him or her out of bed but they will provide moral support and words of encouragement. The child is given a clock to check when he or she can call the supporters back in. The supporters also tell the child they will not come if the child calls them in between the ten-minute intervals but are willing to call out one time from the other room how many minutes are left. If the child tries to go into the supporters' bed in the middle of the night (which is a rare occurrence), the supporters must take the child back to his or her own bed gently and with words of encouragement. Often, the child falls asleep late the first night. The next day, they all get up early and go out on a vigorous day of activity (swimming pool, performance, playdate). The second night the child is in a different situation: tired and more able to sleep in his or her own bed (because it already happened last night). The second night the child always falls asleep much faster. The next day, when the parents come home, it is clear to everyone the child can sleep by himself or herself. All that remains to be done is to incorporate the achievement into the situation when the parents are home.

One situation in which the presence of a support network is critical is in a mass emergency situation, such as war or natural disaster. In such situations, the organization of a group of families to help each other proves itself as one of the primary mechanisms that can prevent post-traumatic reactions. One of the lessons of the home front from Israeli wars is that the attempt to help victims by individual treatment is far less effective than working with families. neighborhoods, or schools. Maintaining social cohesion has proven to be a main factor for both recovery and rehabilitation and one of the best immunizers against mental harm. The greatest harm to a child is caused when, as a result of the state of anxiety, the child is taken out of his or her own circle of interpersonal affiliation. The last thing the child needs is to be put into a quiet corner at home for a long period of time.

Support, Don't Protect

The transition from protecting to supporting is critical for promoting successful coping with anxiety. Parents protect when they try to prevent the child from feeling any experience of anxiety. Parents support when they show they know what the child is going through and gently but firmly push the child toward normal functioning. Supportive principles include showing the child that the parents recognize the child's suffering, encouraging baby steps, being sensitive when pushing the child, and negotiating plan details.

Show the Child That the Parent Recognizes His or Her Suffering

We cannot give support without expressing recognition of the reality of the difficulty faced by the child. Any insinuation that the child is pretending or being manipulative undermines any support proffered. Anxious children really do suffer. Saying to a child "I know you're suffering, and I know your fear is real," does not detract from the child's willingness to cope with it. Actually, the opposite is the typical reaction.

> *Murad, 10, suffered from acute worrying. He worried something would happen to his mom, that he would get diseases, that war would break out, that there would be an earthquake, or even that the sun would go out. Every time he felt fear from one of his worries, he called his mother, Lea.*
>
> *The therapist helped Lea understand that the pattern of phone calls and reassurances was a good example of protectiveness that deepens and perpetuates the anxiety reaction. As a result of this understanding, Lea told her son, "I realize that my talking to you every time you call is not good at all! I know you are really suffering, but talking on the phone dozens of times a day is not the way to support you. From now on, I will not be available by phone during work. You can call John (Lea's boyfriend). He is willing to answer you. When I come home in the evening, we can sit together and talk about how your day was."*
>
> *When Lea got home that evening, she found to her surprise that he had limited himself to two phone calls to John. John's encouragement was infinitely more effective than Lea's reassurances. Murad's worrying declined considerably, and when it did happen, Murad had developed a much better ability to cope with it than before. So had Lea.*

Encourage Baby Steps

Overcoming anxiety almost never happens in one fell swoop. Rather, gradual exposure leads to partial improvement. Therefore, it is important to devise a gradual plan of exposure, with every gain, even the smallest, receiving acknowledgment and encouragement.

In the previous example, where the mother completely stopped accepting her son's calls at work, there were elements of gradation. Murad could get help from his mom's boyfriend, and Lea sat with Murad every evening when she got back from work. The encouragements Murad got from John demonstrated that even the smallest achievement was worthy of commendation.

One of the important elements of effective support is to look for a small achievement and focus on it positively. Anxious children and their parents are used to looking at the empty half of the glass, that is, at the behavior that shows that the child is still anxious. Learning to notice and shed light on the full half of the glass, or even just a full quarter or tenth of the glass, changes the picture.

Billy, 11, was afraid of going up to his bedroom on the second floor of his house. He refused to be there alone even if his father, Jack, talked to him from downstairs. Only when he got up in the morning did he manage to be upstairs alone.

Jack told him, "In the morning, you conquer your fear! You stay upstairs for a few minutes until you finish brushing your teeth and getting dressed. How do you manage to do it?"

Billy answered with his typical sense of humor, "It looks like in the morning the fear hasn't woken up yet!"

This answer was the grounds for a new formula: "We better take fear by surprise before it wakes up!" Together, Jack and Billy planned a surprise offensive on fear. Jack would stand in the room next to the staircase, Billy would run up a few stairs, wait until "fear recovered from the surprise," and then go back down. Jack would count with Billy the number of stairs he went up and time how many seconds it took the fear to recover from the surprise offensive. Jack and Billy drew a graph with two axes, the number of stairs and the number of seconds, to track his progress.

Billy, who was a very competitive child, responded to the game and made progress on both axes. Within a few days, he got to the top step and managed to stay there for half a minute. Billy's grandfather, who lived abroad, emailed him a certificate of achievement, marking Billy's first victory over his fears: standing on the second floor for two whole minutes!

Push Sensitively

Positive encouragement is one side of the support process. The other side is a judicious push for the child to take on an appropriate level of responsibility. The parents' chore in pushing is to make it clear to the child that the parents will no longer step in as they did before. As long as parents continue doing for the child things that the child can really do alone, the child will remain dependent. Some simple rules can help parents avoid common mistakes in this process. First, focus the message on the parents rather than on the child. Focusing on the child, with statements such as "you can do it yourself!" can draw resistance and even present the child with a negative challenge, namely, to prove to the parents that he or she is not capable of accomplishing the task. A simple statement that the parents are going to stop intervening because it does not seem suitable to them will spark less resistance. The child will be able to draw the conclusion that he or she can do it. Alternatively, an outside supporter can help the child develop the necessary capacity to do the job.

Johnny, 10, suffered from social anxiety that made it hard for him to talk with people outside of his immediate family. He was very fond of reading, and his mother, Deborah, drove him to the library once a week. Johnny chose the books, but Deborah was the one who interacted with the librarian while Johnny stood withdrawn at her side.

Once Deborah realized that her services were not helping Johnny but making his problem worse, she told him, "From now on, I am not going to talk to the librarian. It's not appropriate. I will take you to the library, but I will sit at one of the tables and work on my laptop."

Johnny made a face, but when he finished reading the books, he had at home he asked if he could go to library. Deborah took him at the usual time. When Johnny started searching the shelves, she sat down at a table and opened her computer without another word. Johnny looked for a book for a long time. When he had found one, he went up to Deborah and quietly asked her to talk to the librarian for him like she always had. She smiled at him, looked at the books, and praised his choice. She also gave him a small encouraging push toward the librarian. Johnny hesitated for a brief moment but finally went and completed the process of borrowing the books.

One way to inform an anxious child about the cessation of unsuitable support is to make an announcement, as we described in chapter 5. Following is an example of an announcement given verbally and in writing to a girl with night fears and separation anxiety:

> "Mara, we know you suffer very much every time you need to stay home alone, or when it's time to go to bed. We see how hard it is for you at those moments, and how much those fears cripple your life. However, we realize that what we have done so far, by always staying with you and letting you sleep with us in our bed, not only has not helped but has even made things worse. So, we have decided that we are not going to ignore the problem anymore and are not going to surrender to your fears. We are going to act in the following ways: We're going to go out, at first for short periods and then for longer ones; we are not going to let you sleep in our bed; we are not going to keep the problem secret but will tell anyone who can help us. We would be happy to give you any support to deal with your fears, including therapy if you want, but our support will not be expressed by surrendering to your fears.
>
> Signed, your loving parents."

Negotiate Plan Details

An important rule in sound support is that slow progress with the child's cooperation is better than seeking quick progress without cooperation. After the parents inform the child, they will not continue specific kinds of inappropriate support, they can discuss the help the child can receive, for instance from the extended family or a professional. Indeed, suitable therapy can help children overcome anxieties, but it is a mistake for parents to walk back their decision to withdraw inappropriate protection in exchange for the child's willingness to go to therapy. Such an agreement will probably condemn the therapy to failure. Sometimes, it is advisable to bring a supporter into the picture to manage the negotiation over the pace and course of the change. Usually, children negotiate more maturely with a supporter than with their parents.

Jack, 17, developed a deep dependence on his father, Izzy, following a car accident when he was 12. Even though he had completely recovered physically, it was still very hard for Jack to separate from his father every time Izzy had to travel for his work. Before every trip he exerted heavy emotional pressure on his father.

In the first years after the accident, Izzy sharply reduced his travel for work, and Izzy and his wife completely stopped travelling as a couple. Gradually, Jack's parents concluded that this pattern harmed everyone. The two parents informed Jack that they were going to go back to living like normal parents, who can go on vacations together, as well as Izzy going on his work trips.

Jack was angry, shouted at his parents that he could not do it, accused them of not being fair, and left the house with a slam of the door. His parents were familiar with his emotional reactions and understood they came from deep anxiety. They also understood that continuing the present situation would only perpetuate the problem.

A week after the outburst, Izzy gave Jack a written schedule of his travels for the next year. Jack got upset again, but this time his maternal grandfather, who was an important figure in Jack's life, came into the picture. The grandfather told Jack that he would be available to help him deal with his difficulties while Izzy was away. He also proposed that the two of them sit down and plan how Jack could contact his father while he traveled so that he would feel his father was close to him despite the physical distance. Jack refused.

When the first trip got closer, Jack's grandfather repeated his offer. This time Jack agreed to make a reasonable daily plan of contact with both his father and his grandfather.

Izzy went on all of his planned trips. The calls with Jack were at first short and dry, partly because Jack wanted to show his father, he was mad at him, but Izzy knew that the contact with the grandfather was ongoing and positive. By the second trip, a better pattern of communication was created. Within a few months, it was clear that Izzy and Jack managed to change their relationship, and Jack's fears had reached a much more manageable level.

Conclusion

Fears are emotional phenomena that appear to differ completely from behavioral problems such as violence, risk-taking, or delinquent tendencies. Indeed, children who tend toward behavioral problems (sometimes called "externalized problems") are often fundamentally different from children who tend toward anxiety or withdrawal patterns (also called "internalized problems"). However, both patterns present parents with a similar challenge. In both cases, parents need to take a clear position and stand up to the child's emotional outbursts and impulsive actions. In both cases, parents who try to act alone feel they are standing on a less solid foundation than parents who develop a support network. The transition from drifting to determined presence is an unforgettable experience both for parents and children.

The two positions that repeatedly unsettle parents of an anxious child are the tendencies toward protectiveness and demandingness. The protective parent is pulled by the current of the child's anxiety and responds with frightened actions taken to rescue the child. The demanding parent hurts the child with messages of anger and distrust. When one parent is protective and the other demanding, an especially problematic constellation is created. However, once the parents manage to balance this seesaw, the conditions for change begin to emerge. Even when only one parent takes a different position, it can set off a positive process. Anxiety increases in conditions of avoidance and decreases with greater exposure to conditions that evoke anxiety. Parents who embrace this principle can make serious changes in their and their children's lives. They overcome their fear of their child being afraid. They manage to insist more effectively that their child carry on with normal duties. They send a message of trust in the child's abilities. If they are also willing to use a support network, they change the ecology of the anxiety so that instead of the anxiety thriving in an incubator that sustains it, conditions are created for its disappearance.

Review and Application

- Ask yourselves if you are protective parents, who undermine your child's ability to cope.

- Ask yourselves if you are pushed into a demanding position that weakens the child even more.
- Ask yourselves if you are on a marital seesaw, where one of you becomes demanding and the other protective.
- Take a look at the unnecessary things you do for your child that keep your child dependent upon you. Plan how to stop gradually but firmly.
- Ask yourselves, "Do we offer our child a degenerative haven?"
- Ask yourselves, "Am I keeping the problems secret and thereby creating an incubator for them to thrive?"
- Learn how to clarify your position with statements that say "We are going to do this!" instead of statements that say "You have to do this!"
- Give the child the message that you can withstand the child's anxiety without becoming frightened or angry.
- Act to restore the requirement to carry on a normal daily life.
- Remember: "Slow progress with the child's cooperation is better than attempting to achieve rapid progress without cooperation!"
- Try to identify and stop any pointless discussion. The ultimate endpoint is the statement, "This is our duty."
- Create conditions for gradual exposure to the frightening situations.
- Use supporters to add to the child's ability to withstand difficult situations.
- Acknowledge every step forward, even the smallest. Show the child you can see and appreciate those steps.
- Remember: Your standing firm is your child's anchor.

Chapter Seven

School

There are two ways parents can abdicate their responsibility from the moment their child enters the education system: (1) conflict and (2) disengagement. The first is typical of parents who collide with teachers or alternatively with the child about schooling. The second is typical of parents who see the whole realm of school and education as foreign and alien territory. Both tracks undermine parental vigilant care and presence as well as the child's prospects as a student. On the other hand, parents who are able to keep an eye on the child's conduct as a student and cooperate with the teachers strengthen their own status and improve their child's ability to function appropriately at school.

Parent-Teacher Confrontations: One of the Scourges of Our Age

The positive engagement of parents and cooperation with teachers have been proven to be critical factors for academic success, overcoming crises, and preventing school dropout. Conversely, when the engagement becomes militant and takes the form of suspicious and hostile control, the conditions for cooperation disappear. This situation is hazardous for the teacher, the parent, and the child.

Defending one's child is a basic instinct. When they feel their child has been wronged, that the child has been disadvantaged, that the child's needs and difficulties are being misunderstood, let alone when the child is addressed offensively, most parents will rebel. They become yet more willing to fight against the perceived injustice if the teacher suggests they are to blame for the child's problems. Here the instinct to defend the child combines with the instinct for self-defense.

Nonetheless, these basic instincts do not explain why a profound change has occurred in parents' willingness to enter confrontations with teachers in the last few generations. In the past, failing or punishing a child did not cause as much of an uproar as it does now. Something basic has changed in our society's attitude toward teachers. Attacking teachers has become fashionable. These situations obviously hurt teachers and their ability to function, but they may be even more harmful for the children and parents involved.

Even though the criticism of teachers is sometimes justified, sweeping accusations, threats, and attempts to have the teacher removed almost always backfire. Before we specify alternative options, however, let us take a look at the grave damage caused by parent-teacher confrontations.

Parent-Teacher Communication Breaks Down

Confrontations seriously undermine parent-teacher communication. The attacked teacher will correctly assess that the parents will not make positive use of information they are given about their child. To the contrary, the teacher will be afraid that the parents will use the information as proof that the teacher has failed. Under these circumstances, the teacher will prefer to be quiet rather than to share. This vastly reduces the parents' ability to exercise vigilant care.

Attacked teachers will not hesitate to share with the other teachers the bad experience they had with the parents so that a wall of silence might be built surrounding the child's actions not only by the individual teacher but also by the entire school. This is a very bad situation for parental status. Parents lose their ability to see their child's behavior, which is critical for their parental role. For instance, they will not receive a report when their child fails to bring school materials, is late for class, and gets into fights with other children. The parents might only find out how bad the situation is when disclosure becomes completely inevitable. Late disclosure is almost always met by a parent's angry question, "Why didn't you tell me?" These parents forget that they have contributed with their own hands to this situation by attacking the teacher in the past.

Parents Become Less Able to Exercise Vigilant Care

The inevitable harm to parental vigilance following confrontations with the teacher deepens the child's problems. Parental vigilant care is the critical factor to prevent harmful processes such as bad company, destructive temptations, and dropping out of school. Parent-teacher confrontations increase those risks. The hostility or disengagement that arise following a confrontation also worsens the child's behavior problems. The reason is simple: Children understand that communication between the parents and teachers has been cut off so now they feel they have nothing to fear at home even if they misbehave crassly at school.

Teachers Become Suspicious and Hostile

Another kind of harm occurs in the teacher's attitude toward the child. Teachers are only human. When they are attacked by parents, the offense they feel is to some extent projected onto the child. There may be many teachers who are able to treat a child fairly and impartially despite the parents' attack, but not everyone is up to the task.

The Child is Immunized to the Consequences of his or her Actions

Also, when parents complain to a principal about a teacher, the negative consequences usually outweigh the hoped-for gains. Sometimes, parents receive momentary satisfaction from the principal calling the teacher to order, scolding the teacher, and reversing the teacher's decision (about grades, disciplinary measures, or easements), but subduing the teacher does not solve the problems. Rather, makes them worse. Now, the child is labeled as having aggressive parents. Other teachers, too, might agree with this assessment.

A common negative scenario is when the principal joins with the parent against the teacher. The child then feels protected from above and as a result feels free to do whatever he or she wants. There are few situations that so quickly and surely lead to the student's deterioration like the feeling of being immune to the consequences of his or her actions.

In Sum

The destructive consequences of parent-teacher confrontations make these situations a veritable educational disaster. Yet, many parents feel they have no choice. In fact, they do have a choice. They can act in such a way that their child's condition and their parental status improve considerably.

Parents & Teachers: A Necessary Alliance

From the moment the child enters the education system, a revolutionary change occurs in the status of both parents and child. From now on, the parents do not have exclusive responsibility for raising the child but have a partner. From now on, the teacher and the parent are in the same boat and only if they row in the same direction will the boat move forward.

It turns out that an honest and respectful appeal for cooperation tends to be "contagious" and draw a positive response from the other side. To facilitate this process, we developed a series of principles for "parent-teacher diplomacy." Some parents smile when they hear the need for diplomacy. Indeed, diplomacy is needed whenever there is a mutual interest as well as areas of potential conflict. Diplomacy is needed when attempting to overcome disengagement, estrangement, or crisis. The main principles of parent-teacher diplomacy include shared understanding, respect for teachers' needs, positive involvement, honesty, addressing communication problems, and small improvements.

Shared Understanding: "We are in the same boat!"

One of the main obstacles to parent-teacher cooperation is the sense of antagonism that pits each side against the other. In many cases, when a parent and teacher meet about a child's problem behavior, there is a sense of criticism in the air. Even a seemingly innocent question or comment such as "why didn't you tell us sooner?" or "We never have such problems at home" can put the teacher on guard as if his or her competence were being questioned by the parents. When the teacher makes matters worse, such as by saying, "I actually did report it twice in the feedback, but I never got a response," the parties are on a collision course. Therefore, it is never a bad idea to lay out a common interest at the beginning of the dialogue with statements such as, "If we act in coordination, I'm sure we'll make progress" or "I have no doubt that you are trying to help my child even if it isn't always easy." When parents manage to open the conversation by giving the teacher credit for his or her goodwill and offering to cooperate, the teacher will usually respond in the same vein.

Sometimes, parents ask us why it is their job rather than the teacher's to open positively. Our answer is clear: It is in the interest of both sides. Later on, in the conversation, it is still wise to reiterate the point of common interest, such as "I would appreciate if sometimes you could also tell me about positive events in the class. Then I can tell my daughter you told me, and she will understand that you noticed her and that we're in constant contact. It will help us all!" Such statements are like grease for the mechanism of the teacher-parent relationship. They facilitate coordination and prevent creaking.

Respect the Teacher's Needs

One source of conflict between parents and teachers is that for the parent, their child is always at the center, whereas the teacher must take care of a whole class. Often, parents ask teachers to give their child special treatment, which might make things hard for a teacher in relation to the other students. Indeed, children with special needs need special treatment but without undermining the teacher's treatment of the whole class. A case in point is coping with a student with ADHD. The teacher must take into account both the child's difficulties and the rest of the class's needs. This is the teacher's job, but this situation makes it very difficult. If the parent ignores that and addresses only the teacher's duties and not their difficulties as well, the dialogue will suffer. This can be prevented if parents show they recognize the teacher's constraints, such as, "It's important to find a way to help my child function better despite her difficulties without hurting the whole class!" Now, the parent is addressing their and the teacher's common interest. This opens the way for the teacher to take a constructive attitude toward the child's special needs.

Positive Involvement

The parent's initial contact with the teacher at the beginning of the school year can have a significant impact on subsequent cooperation. The first parent-teacher conference is an opportunity to begin a year-long dialogue on the right foot. It is an opportunity to show the teacher a willingness to help if and when a problem arises. A good way to do it is to mention the importance of sharing information such as, "I would appreciate if you tell me what's happening whether good or bad. It will help me be helpful!"

Parents should prepare for their first meeting with the teacher by asking their child about his or her experiences at the beginning of the school year. The parent can ask their child to see class materials for different subjects and ask the child about the first things they did in class. Even little things can pave the way for positive relations with the teacher. For instance, "I understand you're teaching decimal fractions; I think my son is starting to get it!" Or "my daughter came home happy the first week. I have a good feeling about the atmosphere in the classroom!" By sharing their first impressions with the teacher, parents show they are interested and involved. This increases the chances the teacher will take the same approach.

Honesty

Speak honestly about the child's problems. One of the common traps that undermine all cooperation is the tendency to deny or minimize the child's problems. Parents do this to protect the child's reputation, prevent labeling, or fend off the threat of transfer to a special school. However, when the parents deny or minimize the child's problems, the implicit message is: "It's not my child's problem but yours!" It would be hard to think of a more problematic message for the parent-teacher relationship.

It is completely different when parents say, "We are well aware of our child's difficulties. We will do everything we can to help." This position promotes constructive dialogue. When the parents are willing to speak openly and offer their help to find a common solution, teachers show more patience and tolerance toward the child. The parents' honesty opens the door for constructing a joint program to help the child succeed in school.

Addressing Communication Problems

Make an effort to bridge communication problems. Conflict or disconnection between the parent and teacher can have serious implications for all sides. When we're angry, we tend to believe the burden of making amends belongs to the other side. The problem is that that's what the other side thinks, too. The rift remains in place, and the damages pile up.

One way to bridge over difficulties is to seek help from a figure with a schoolwide function such as principal, advisor, or head teacher. Parents must approach them with the intention of mending the rift, not in order to settle accounts with the teacher. When a parent suggests mediation, it is not rare for the teacher to show willingness not only to improve but also to apologize for any part in the problem.

We must remember that in many cases the parents have also said harsh words in the heat of conflict. Therefore, an act of goodwill from them as well would be appropriate. In the distant past, parents brought teachers a token gift, either at the beginning of the school year or to help relieve tensions: the mythical apple. There are cartoons about schools showing a teacher softly gazing at an apple she just received. Maybe we need something to fill the place of the traditional apple. One option is to bring the teacher or principal a copy of this book. All sides would benefit, including me.

Small Improvements

A small improvement in the alliance with the teacher can go a long way. There are different levels of cooperation that can be reached with different teachers. Only some teachers, or rather, some teacher-parent pairs, can reach full cooperation.

In most cases, cooperation will be only partial, but even limited cooperation is immeasurably better than disconnection, let alone conflict. We can draw a spectrum of levels of cooperation, from worst to best. We believe the level of cooperation can always be raised by at least one notch. Even a modest improvement can have significant consequences, among other reasons because improvements in the relationship with one teacher tend to spread to other teachers and cause a cumulative positive effect. We suggest that every parent try to rate their relationship with teachers and other functionaries (advisor, principal, vice principal) by the following scale:

(-2) anger and mutual accusation

(-1) lack of contact

(0) formal relations

(+1) willingness to report to each other

(+2) willingness to help

(+3) full cooperation

When parents use the principles of parent-teacher diplomacy, they can improve their relationships with each teacher and each staff member by at least one degree. Positive contacts tend to impact not only the relationship with that person but also with others. Thus, a modest improvement in one relationship will also project on other relationships.

Vivian was Rafi's teacher in sixth and seventh grades. She was familiar with his learning and attention issues but also knew how to task him and monitor his behavior. The combination of supervision and support enabled Rafi to function well despite his difficulties.

However, because of changes in the school, Rafi started eighth grade with new teachers who didn't know him. An introvert, Rafi began to withdraw in class. His grades dropped, and he started to isolate himself from others. His deterioration, though, was not obvious because he was a quiet student. The combination of a new staff and particularly quiet behavior made him invisible. Only a few months later did his parents realize he was in trouble. He flunked some subjects, stopped socializing with his classmates, and dropped out of the school basketball team.

Rafi also started to deteriorate emotionally, and there was concern he was sinking into depression. In her distress, his mother, Mira, called his former teacher, Vivian, and related the whole chain of events to her. Vivian said, "Rafi is one of those kids who, when not seen, feel as if they don't exist!"

Vivian held a conversation with Dore, Rafi's new teacher. Dore and Vivian agreed that Vivian would tutor Rafi in the subjects in which his grades dropped. Later Dore served as a connection between Vivian and the specialist teachers, who showed a willingness to pay attention both to Rafi's difficulties and his achievements.

Vivian's return to the picture quickly improved Rafi's morale. The fact that some of the teachers started to pay attention to him, even in passing, eased his feeling of disappearing. Within a month from the beginning of the intervention, there were no longer signs of depression, Rafi came out of his seclusion and performed better in school. His mother's situation also improved. Mira felt she had partners in the school whom she could turn to if necessary.

Vigilant Care and Support

Vigilant care is a flexible position: the desirable level of involvement should be matched to the child's academic performance and emotional situation. When the child is performing well as a student and there are no signs of danger, the parent should show interest and keep an eye on the child but from a distance that enables the child to study and adjust independently. When children struggle, they should be supported. When they get in trouble, parents should closely check what is going on. If they are in danger, parents should take determined action to protect them and get them out of the trouble they are in. These challenges continue from kindergarten through graduation.

What a Parent Needs to Know

Parents who show interest quickly get a picture of their child's academic and behavioral functioning, his or her social situation and state of mind in relation to school. Even when the child gets older, it is critical for parents to have a picture of these areas of the child's life in order to notice problems in advance and be able to intervene in time.

To tighten their vigilant care after signs of decline appear, parents can check homework on a regular basis, increase the frequency of their contact with the teachers, and find out about school materials and test dates as well as whether their child has been late, absent or had other disciplinary problems. This knowledge is critical for the parents' ability to support their child and prevent the child from falling back. Parents ask what to do if their child resists the tightening of their vigilant care. We suggest they give their child the following message: "As long as there were no special problems, I didn't check or investigate. But certain things happened lately that make me concerned (give examples). These are signs of trouble. It is my duty to check more closely and do everything I can to keep you safe."

Most children accept this position in their hearts, even if they protest. Many children protest even when deep in their hearts they justify their parents' positions.

How to Be Supportive Rather than Protective

When a child has functional problems, the challenge for parents is to be supportive but not protective. A supportive parent helps their child function better as a student. Whereas a protective parent takes the responsibility off the child as a student. Here are some examples of protectiveness in relation to school:

- The parent finishes the child's homework.
- The parent provides false excuses or notes for the child's truancy or failure to complete homework.
- The parent arranges the child's school bag for them.
- The parent lets the child stay home when it is hard for him or her to go to school.

And here are examples of support rather than protectiveness:

- The parent sits down with the child and helps complete the assignments that are difficult for the child, but insists that the child also practice on his or her own.
- The parent tells the child they will help to deal with the difficulties but not give excuses for failures.
- The parent helps the child explain his or her difficulties to the teacher, but insists that the child be part of this process and that the information be credible.
- The parent shows understanding for the child's organizational difficulties and sits with the child when he or she arranges the schoolbag.
- The parent helps look for a solution for the child's difficulties in school but makes it clear the child cannot stay home.

In the examples of protectiveness, the parent carries the child on their back and thereby gives them the message that they don't expect anything of the child. Alternatively, the parent signals that they cannot withstand the child's pressures. In an attempt to prevent discomfort for the child or for themselves, protective parents lose their anchoring.

The Difference between Tightening Vigilant Care and Imposing Sanctions

Tightening the vigilant care of a misbehaving child is a powerful measure with often very unpleasant consequences that differ radically from regular sanctions. In a routine sanction, the message is: "If you behave badly, you will be punished!" And when the child is punished, the implicit message is: "I told you so!" These are messages of control. Such messages are unbearable for many children, especially the stubborn and rebellious ones. Such children feel that in order to maintain their honor they must continue their problem behavior despite the threat or punishment. Thus, the punishment achieves the opposite outcome of that intended.

Surprisingly, the same paradox occurs when stubborn or rebellious children are rewarded for good behavior. These children might feel that if they change their behavior as a result of the reward, they are indicating that the adult can "buy" them. They must prove they are not for sale. As long as they have not proved that, their honor balance remains negative. This is not the case when the adult gives the child the message, "It is my duty to watch you closely so you do not hurt others or get hurt!" The message is particularly effective when it is free of insinuations of control. Fingers are not pointed with threats or blame. With their voice, body and words, the adult announces, "It is my duty to protect you! I am not going to give up on you!"

Many parents react to this suggestion by saying, "But for him it is exactly like a punishment!" Indeed, the child experiences the tightening of vigilant care as an unpleasant move, to say the least. But the parents' locus of control is themselves and not the child. An increased presence demonstrates the parent's commitment to the child's best interest, and the child feels it even when protesting. A normal sanction is like attempted remote control. The child does not feel supported, does not feel the parent's commitment, and does not feel intimacy. The opposite is true in tightened vigilant care. Therefore, tightening vigilant care is much more than a sanction.

The positive force of vigilant care is particularly felt when parents and teachers join forces. When parents and teachers agree on a plan to tighten supervision of some aspect of the child's behavior, they strengthen their status, give their child a sense of accompaniment, reduce risks, and usually induce a significant improvement in the child's performance. Throughout the process, the only "sanction" is that both the parents and the teachers keep a close eye on the child and sit with the child frequently for debriefing, provide support and encouragement, and plan steps for future improvement.

How to contribute to the success of meetings with the school staff

It is not easy for parents to get called to meet the school staff, especially when it occurs as a result of their child's serious behavior problems. The parents feel, sometimes justifiably, that the staff are angry and accusatory. They are afraid of painful outcomes such as the child's being sent to a special school. Sometimes, they also feel powerless in light of the staff's expectation that they set things right and discipline their child. Many children who talk back, refuse to do as they are asked, or have angry outbursts at school do the same thing at home. No wonder the parents feel frustrated by the staff's expectations! How can they exercise their authority over the child at school if they can't even do it at home?

Positive Messaging

The school meeting can be a positive turning point. Parents can help this happen if they prepare in advance and take a few simple steps. They can give the staff a message that will reduce suspicion and increase prospects of cooperation, e.g., "Before we begin, we want to say that this meeting is very important to us. We want to hear about the problems and want to help. We hope we leave here with a joint plan."

This message might surprise the staff, especially if there were previously problematic interactions between them and the parents. This message, even if it makes some teachers raise their eyebrows, can increase openness and reduce suspicion.

Sometimes, it is hard for parents to offer such a positive message because they are angry at the school for the way it is handling the problem or even for inviting them to the meeting. But remember that an atmosphere of anger might not only undermine the meeting but also harm the child. Therefore, it is in the parents' interest to make an effort to steer the meeting toward cooperation.

Transparency

Parents should let their child know about the meeting. They should maintain an objective tone with their child. They might tell their child, "We were called in to a meeting at school. You are our child, and we are going to school to help you! But it is very important for us to cooperate with the teachers. We are sure such cooperation will be good for you, too!"

This statement clarifies to the child that the parents are on his or her side, but that does not mean they are against the teacher. This neutralizes a common trap in the parent-teacher-child triangle, which is making the relationship a power struggle in which the child incites the parents against the teachers. It is even worse when the parents incite the child against the teacher.

Prioritization

A successful meeting enables parents and teachers to zoom in on a few particularly problematic issues in the child's behavior. To achieve the desirable focus, they must prioritize: select two or no more than three specific problem behaviors, against which the parents and teachers agree to work together. In many cases, the child's problems are described in general or vague terms that prevent effective action. Phrases such as "unmotivated," "low self-esteem," "restless," or "social difficulties" are too general and do not provide traction for a practical plan. It is also usually harmful to try to put a psychological label on the child's problems.

Parents can prevent diverting the discussion and aim it in constructive directions, for example, they can say something like "The issue of our child's diagnosis is important, and we will consider it seriously. But we would like not to miss the opportunity we have now to focus on his main problem behaviors and come out of here with a joint plan. This will help us all deal better with the burning issues. Why don't we try to define the most problematic behaviors that bother us all?"

This request is very hard to refuse, and in this way, parents can influence the conduct and outcome of the meeting even if they did not initiate it or set its agenda. When parents show a desire to cooperate and honestly address "the most problematic behaviors that bother *us all*," they gain positive influence over the direction of the meeting.

It should be noted that a lot depends on tone of voice. The more respectful the tone, the better chances of the request leading to the desired result.

Some teachers find it hard to focus on one or two main problems, partly because of the feeling that the child challenges them in other ways as well. For instance, after one participant suggests focusing on the child's walking out of class without permission and talking back to teachers, another teacher might ask, "But what about the constant chatter?" Or" what about him being late?" And on and on.

Here, too, the parents can have a positive effect. For instance, they can reply, "Just because we decide to focus on two main issues, it doesn't mean you have to stop working on the other problems. You do what you need to do so that you can keep teaching. Here, we would like to make a joint program that will enable us to work together. To do so, we should focus on the main issues. This will help us support you better."

Recruiting Partial Support

Parents often expect the entire staff to work together and go along with the prioritization of the problem behaviors. Even though such an expectation is understandable, it can undermine the action plan. Teachers cannot always act in concert because of the natural differences between them. Therefore, it is recommended for the parents to suggest to the teacher to recruit one or two more staff members who have been facing similar problems. Here, too, the selective focus strengthens rather than weakening movement toward the desired outcome. The desire to achieve complete uniformity undermines the possibility of achieving partial but meaningful cooperation. Recruiting support within the staff is always partial, and striving to achieve an absolutely uniform approach misses the mark.

Phone Calls

After prioritizing, it is advisable to propose a daily phone call for a limited time period between the teacher and parents. Parents should suggest it in a way that shows they respect the teacher and appreciate the time it will require. We recommend a 3-week period of daily contact (after which they move to communication on an as-needed basis). It is important for the communication to be personal and not take place only through voice mail. Following is an example of a respectful proposal by the parents: "To enable us to be the most helpful, how would you like to be in daily contact for three weeks? We don't want to be a burden so we will accept any way that you propose. Sometimes, just a few words will be enough for us to be mutually updated, to show our child we are in the picture and working together. What would be the most convenient for you?" This is a modest and respectful request. The parents convey to the staff that they are on their side and seeking a way to help and be helped in the most effective and economic way.

Positive Events

It is important for the parent-teacher communication to also include positive events. For instance, the parents might tell the teacher: "Gil came home with a good feeling about his math class." Or "Shirley was proud to tell us she worked well with some of her classmates on preparing the holiday performance." When problematic events occur, parents are instructed to tell their child that they talked to the teacher, know about what happened, and are going to think together about a suitable response, e.g., "We know you hit a girl in your class today. We are going to think with your teacher about how to make sure this doesn't happen again!"

Parents should have a weekly talk with their child to go over the events of the last week. They should subsequently update the teacher about the talk and its conclusions. Sometimes, the parent who was not in touch with the teacher in the past ought to make the call. For many children, it comes as a complete surprise that their parents and teachers are coordinating. If the father was less involved in the past, his calls may be of special importance. One of the fathers we advised reported with a smile, "My calling the teacher was a real 'constructive trauma' for my son. He was astonished!"

Concluding the Meeting

The best way to conclude the school conference is by an announcement to the child of the decisions that were made. The parents can suggest to the teacher that they do it together. There is special value in the parents' and teacher's calling the child into the room together and telling the child that they have agreed to cooperate in firm and coordinated resistance to the problem behaviors. Following are two examples of announcements, one read by the teacher in the parents' presence, and the other made by the parents at home:

(1) "We have gathered here, I and your parents because there have been certain behaviors in the past few weeks, we have decided we will not accept. We decided together with your parents to firmly resist verbal abuse of the teachers and your leaving class without permission. Your parents and I will be in daily contact about this and, if necessary, will involve additional staff members. We care about you so we are not going to give up on you or let you have your own way."

(2) "We and the school staff sat down together to find a way to stop your walking around the classroom during class and coming to school without the right equipment. We decided together to watch you closely and maintain ongoing contact between us. We are sure you can overcome your difficulties. We will do everything to help you succeed!"

When parents prepare for the meeting and apply the principles we described, chances of success increase steeply. Surprisingly, a meeting that at first seemed burdensome can turn out to be an opening for improvement. It is not for nothing that we presented the description of our plan for the school meeting directly after the discussion of teacher-parent diplomacy. Diplomatic wisdom is precisely the art of preventing possible breakdowns and getting the most out of meetings. Such meetings often begin with a sense of crisis. The Chinese character indicating the word "crisis" is the same symbol that indicates "opportunity." The approach we described for school meetings is designed precisely to turn a crisis into an opportunity.

Difficulty Getting Ready for School

Many parents experience getting ready for school in the morning as a war of attrition. Often, they get to work exhausted and irritable. For many children, it is hard to get up in the morning, get out of bed, get dressed, prepare their school bag, and stick to the timetable. Parents' pressure can add a layer of irritability that makes things worse. The positive involvement of parents who are willing to supervise and support their children can make things better.

Morning difficulties have a special significance. If the day begins with a relatively relaxed feeling instead of an experience of chaos, the child and parents leave the home in a good mood and with more strength for the day's challenges. Besides, successful morning preparation creates a model that can be used in other situations.

We suggest making morning preparation the first goal of improvement in families where it is a problem. The best way is to break down the morning preparations into sub-tasks, for each one of which parents provide supervision and support. Parental presence is expressed by the parent's willingness to accompany the child from the suitable distance for each sub-task. Support is shown by the parent's willingness to help as long as the child also does something on his or her own at each and every stage. Breaking the morning tasks into sub-tasks helps parents identify the sources of difficulty, specify the situations that require help, and decide where the pace should be slowed down.

It is advisable to start the night before by going over the schedule and preparing the school bag, clothes. and sandwiches. You can tell the child, "We decided to help you get ready for school better in the morning. We know it's hard for you to remember everything and do everything alone, especially in the morning, when you're not completely awake. So, we're going to start getting ready the night before. Every night we're going to go over your schedule with you, help you prepare your bag, choose your clothes, and make your sandwich." It is important for the child to take some responsibility for each task. For instance, you go over the schedule together and ask the child to get the appropriate books and notebooks out. You choose clothes together. Ask the child to put them on the chair. Give your child a suitable job in preparing the sandwich. At each stage, the parent should supervise and support but the child should participate.

In cases where one parent usually deals alone with complex morning preparations, we suggest making changes in responsibility delegation. The father's entry into some of the roles that were previously the exclusive responsibility of the mother, or vice-versa, can be an opening for change. Even if the father leaves the house early in the morning, he can be involved in tasks the night before. If it is done in good spirit, the child will find the father's image present in his or her mind in the morning. The fact that the father performs preparation tasks with the child ahead of the morning gives the mother broader shoulders. The mother might be physically alone with the child in the morning, but now she represents both parents. Sometimes, such cooperation is possible even when the parents are divorced. For instance, the father can talk to the child on the phone at night and go over the morning plan with the child.

During the intervention to change morning routines, parents should wake up half an hour earlier than usual. This changes the sense of stress. We also recommend removing distractors such as computer, TV or cell phone use in the morning. The child should be informed in advance, and measures should be taken to prevent turning on those devices.

In the case of adolescents, implementation might require additional tools, such as introducing supporters. For some adolescents, the involvement of a teacher can be a positive critical event. In several cases we treated, change occurred after a teacher made a house call to talk to the child about the morning preparation problems. In one case, the teacher announced she was going to stop at a boy's house in the morning on her way to school. Once a principal came to a 16-year-old girl's house and woke her up from sleep. In two cases of ninth-grade boys, twelfth-grade girls agreed to stop by their houses in the morning as part of the social project they were leading. In all of those cases, one visit was enough to create a change and cut off a pattern of lateness.

Bullying

One of the biggest concerns of all parents is that their child will fall victim to bullying. It is a common mistake to think that bullying is simply a discipline problem. Parents complain to the school expecting that the bully will be severely punished and that this will solve the problem. On the other side of the picture are the parents of the child accused of bullying, claiming that the problem has been blown out of proportion and that the school took unjust measures. The truth is that punishing is not an effective solution to this problem. Bullies continue to harass others even after punishments of long suspension. Meanwhile, the victim does not feel any safer because now they are also afraid of the bully's revenge. Sometimes, schools rely on educational talks with the class, but the problem of such talks is that they tend to persuade only the children who were already persuaded in the first place. Many bullies remain unimpressed.

Ron, 14, was anxious and withdrawn. He was transferred to a special class because a year earlier his school was concerned about his signs of depression. In his new class he quickly became the victim of systematic harassment, including "friendly" back slaps, by a group of children who competed with each other in hitting him behind the teacher's back. Ron was afraid to say who was hitting him because he was afraid it would make matters worse.

Ron's mother understood he was the victim of bullying, and she went to the teacher twice, but she could not identify the culprits. When Ron's mother questioned him about his problem, he said: "There's nothing to do about it. They just wait for the teacher to turn around to the board, and then they hit me; and in a split second they're back in their seats as if nothing happened!"

Ron is actually telling us, "I'm not seen!" His wish to be seen can only arouse sympathy. But what can you do that if the bullies are nimble and elusive? Indeed, as long as you look for a way to catch the culprits red-handed, it seems like a mission impossible.

The deeper meaning of supervision (both by parents and teachers) is not about catching the culprits but creating an experience of accompaniment. Children feel accompanied when the adults act in a way that conveys the message, "You are important to us. We can see you. We are thinking about you." In this situation, the children stop feeling abandoned to their fate. The experience of supervision and accompaniment is the critical factor, even when you do not manage to expose all of the details of the problematic events.

Yves, 10, was a new student. Even though he was popular at his previous school, he became the victim of daily harassment at his new school.

He was tormented mainly by Dylan, a child with a high social status in the class, who would greet him in the morning with a clap on his head. Sometimes, he invited other children to join in.

Gabe, Yves' father, noticed his son was going to school unwillingly, which had never happened before. When Gabe asked if something was wrong, Yves gave an evasive answer. When this happened again, Gabe sat his son down for a talk and said, "I can tell something is wrong. Please, don't say it's nothing because I know that's not true. I know you very well, and I know when something bad is happening to you."

This time Yves reacted differently. He could feel his father was "seeing him," which means looking at him caringly and noticing something was wrong. This feeling enabled him to tell his father he was being hit and to tell him who was doing it. But he begged his father not tell the teacher because that would be tattling and he by no means wanted to be seen as a tattletale.

Gabe promised he would do everything to handle the problem without telling the teacher who was harassing him. But despite this constraint, Gabe acted to create an atmosphere of supervision. First, he called Dylan's mother. He told her that Yves had asked him not to tell the teacher Dylan's name. He asked the mother to tell that to her son. He added that if both parents cooperated, they might be able to solve the problem in the best way for Dylan as well. This attitude helped Dylan's mother be willing to cooperate, which would not have been the case had Gabe talked to her in an accusing tone. Dylan's mother told Gabe she would report to him about her conversation with her son.

Subsequently, more than one conversation was needed between Gabe and Dylan's mother. The mother's initial intervention led to one week of calm, but then Dylan went back to hitting Yves. This time Gabe was not satisfied with a phone call but asked to personally meet both of Dylan's parents. He said he was going to tell the teacher that Yves was suffering from systematic harassment, but he would respect his son's request not to disclose the name of the boy who was harassing him. The parents undertook to make it clear to their son that they took the situation seriously. They promised to keep a daily eye on developments.

Gabe spoke to the teacher and told her about his conversations with the parents but kept his promise not to identify the harassing boy. The teacher initiated a class activity in which she talked about certain children suffering from repeated harassment. She said she was following the situation closely and was already in touch with several parents. Now Yves, Dylan, and the rest of the class felt they were being watched closely.

At a parent-teacher conference two weeks later, the teacher reported to the class's parents that there had been cases of bullying in the class but the alertness of some parents led to an effective handling of the problem. She asked the parents to pay attention to any sign that their child was not feeling comfortable in the class. In such a case she asked them to let her know immediately so she could watch more closely and give the children adequate protection.

Parents might be surprised by the sincere willingness to cooperate both by the parents of the harassing boy and by the teacher. Indeed, in many cases when parents make a complaint they are met with less positive reactions by other parents and teachers, who react with doubt and impatience toward the complaining parent. We think there are two reasons for the cooperation in this case:

a. The father spoke respectfully, without accusation and without demanding drastic disciplinary solutions. Both when he called the parents and the teacher, his message was, "If we cooperate, we will find a good solution for everyone." This message increases the willingness to help whereas an angry and blaming message would have achieved the opposite outcome.

b. The father offered a clear direction for joint action. The message to the parents and the teacher was, "If it is clear to the children that we are watching and keeping an eye on them, they will feel differently." The offer of constructive action improved the cooperation of both the parents and the teacher whereas demanding disciplinary action might have led to a very different reaction.

There is an increased chance of cooperation if the parents of the bullied child talk to the parents of the offending child even when that child denies the bullying or explains it as "just joking around." If the child claims, for example, that he or she is always falsely blamed, the parents can say,

"We will be watching closely, and will see if that turns out to be true." The decision to keep a close eye usually becomes the best way to avoid false accusations, but it also requires the bullying child to show self-restraint.

This process often depends on the willingness of the teachers to be involved in this way. Parents cannot dictate the teachers' desired behavior, but it is hard for a teacher to refuse a positive and respectful request by a parent, especially if it is supported by several parents. Creating a joint parents' initiative is often within the reach of concerned parents. The first step is for the parents of the bullied child to ask their child if there are other children who are being bullied as well. A child who feels their parents' genuine concern will be willing to share that information with them. When the parents approach the parents of other children who are also being bullied, it creates a group that is willing to join hands. The fact that the parents propose a constructive solution such as increasing the joint supervision by parents and teachers strengthens their hand in relation to the school. In this situation, even the principal will not be indifferent.

Truancy

School absenteeism develops gradually. At first, children miss a few days or maybe just a few classes. Then, the absences start to appear in succession and sometimes end with an all-out refusal to go to school. Children who frequently skip school days gradually lose their identity as students. That identity is the child's basic feeling that his or her main role is to study and go to school. In the vast majority of cases, children take for granted that they are students. The identity of student gives them clarity, stability, and belonging. When the absences pile up, that identity begins to weaken. A problematic alternative identity begins to replace it. For instance, the child might perceive him or herself as a failure, sick or marginal. Those children's reference group also changes, such as when they begin to see themselves primarily as members of a street gang, a group of children addicted to a particular online game, or the population of dropouts and misfits. Some children try to adopt a positive imaginary identity, sometimes an outsized one. These children fantasize that they actually have unique talents, hidden abilities, or a creativity that is not understood by others. The more their functioning in reality withers, the greater the gap between their image and their ability.

Maintaining and restoring the child's identity as a student has to involve real action by responsible adults and not only an attempt to achieve an internal emotional change in the child. Therefore, psychotherapy for the child that is not accompanied by practical steps will fail to restore the child's identity as a student. Only if the therapy includes clear measures to end the child's staying at home and a practical plan to go back to school will it provide real help.

In case the child stays at home, parents can take measures to prevent the emergence of problematic habits. The parents must make sure that the child wakes up at the normal time. It is important that school hours not fill up with leisure activities like going out with friends or looking at screens. Sometimes, when the problem is in its inception, parents are not prepared to prevent activities like watching television or becoming glued to computer screens. But as soon as the absences begin to repeat, parents must make sure that the rules are maintained. Therefore, it is best for the child not to stay home alone. Parents can get help from family members (grandparents can do this if the rules are explained to them) or take their child to work with them if possible. During work, it is important not to turn the day into a party but to provide conditions for doing school work. Sometimes, parents ask whether such solutions won't make the problem worse by giving the child attention. From our experience, if the parent is careful not to make spending the day together fun, taking the child to work can be an appropriate initial response.

A basic principle for treating truancy is creating early contact with the school. Sometimes, parents are tempted to give an excuse for the truancy, such as when an anxious child is afraid of the teacher's reaction to mistakes, or when both the child and the parents are afraid the child's grades will suffer. Such solutions reinforce the tendency to be truant and undermine the relationship with the teachers. Therefore, it is necessary to report the real reason for the truancy to the teacher. Honesty enables construction of a joint program to give the child the best chances to overcome the problem.

When the problem recurs several times, the parents should not only report by phone but also have a meeting with the teacher to figure out how to tighten vigilant care. For the child, just knowing that the parents and school are mutually informed and coordinated is a step toward solving the problem. A meeting with the teacher also allows joint exploration of the factors or events at school that might be related to the child's difficulties. For instance, the parent might bring up the child's complaints about bullying by other children or difficulties in a certain subject. The teacher can provide information based on direct observation or prepare for close supervision to find out what is bothering the child.

When a truant child can't do homework alone and the parents can't sit with him or her in the morning, they can do so in the evening. It is important not to reach bedtime without the child having touched his or her schoolwork and the parents having been updated on the day's assignments. If the parents can't sit with the child or help with the homework, they should look for a supporter who can do it in their place. Sometimes, the school can help, such as a classmate bringing the child the day's homework and helping the child to do it. A school that prepares to handle truancy can involve students from higher grades, for instance as part of a community service assignment. These measures can steeply reduce the risk that truancy develop into all-out avoidance

Conclusion

Parents should stay on top of their child's situation at school. To that end, they should maintain positive communication with the teachers. The level of parental involvement is determined by the child's performance level. When the child meets assigned responsibilities to a reasonable extent, parents can accompany the child from a distance. They are happy to see the child's school books once in a while, look at the child's report card together, and catch up with the teacher occasionally. If it turns out that the child is neglecting or struggling with schoolwork, parents should tighten their vigilance, check school assignments together daily with the child, and maintain ongoing contact with the teacher to keep each other informed. When parents approach teachers respectfully and propose a way to increase vigilant care, there is a good chance they will be met with openness. Disconnection and confrontation with teachers not only undermine the status of both the parents and the teachers but seriously undermines the child's performance.

Review and Application

- Show the child you're interested in his or her academic and social situation. Ask yourselves, "Do I know who my child's friends are in the class, what material they are learning, what the difficulties are?"

- Try to make contact with the parents of some of your child' classmates.
- Maintain good relations with the teachers. If a problem arises, look for a way to settle it.
- Homework is an important window through which you can accompany your child at school. Keep yourself informed on a regular basis.
- If you feel that morning preparation is problematic and exhausting, make a plan to help you start the day on the right foot. Break down the tasks into sub-tasks, do some of them the night before, and support your child in a way that helps acquire the necessary organizational skills.
- When you come to the teacher or principal with a respectful request, the chances of a positive response are high.
- Bullying is not merely a disciplinary problem. The demand for severe punishment does not serve your child.
- Be aware of signs of truancy.
- The immediate response to truancy is to create a plan of joint supervision with teachers.
- In all contacts with teachers, remember, "We are in the same boat!"
- Wherever your child is facing a difficulty, remember, "Support, don't protect!"

Chapter Eight

Screens

Co-authored with Yaron Sela and Merav Zach

Of all the causes of drifting that face children in our generation, none is as ubiquitous as the smartphone. The role of the smartphone in their lives is so powerful that it can be referred to as "another family member." The smartphone is present in almost every encounter between children and their parents and between children and their friends, but it plays a different role in those two situations. When children are with their peers, the smartphone often serves as a social glue. The primary author of this book was recently sitting on a train that was full of teenagers who had just got out of school. All the kids who were sitting together and talking to each other were holding open smartphones in their hands. In their group conversations, some of the time the children were speaking directly to each other and some of the time showing each other their smartphone screens. It was evident that the device contributed to the communication and helped fill the dead moments while providing content for further communication. The children did not get lost in their smartphones but used them to share with each other. This is not the case when children are with their parents. All it takes is a quick glance at families sitting around tables at restaurants. The smartphone almost always separates and isolates people from each other: the children are absorbed in their phones, far from the shared world with their parents.

Parents feel a particularly deep helplessness when it comes to the virtual world. In addition to the usual difficulties with different influences on their children, they also have a sense of technological inferiority compared to their children. Children's skills in the virtual world are usually far superior to their parents'. The relationship between parents and children in the virtual realm has been likened to that between tourists and natives. For parents, this world is relatively foreign; they look at it from the outside and feel clumsy with it whereas the child is at home in the virtual reality, navigates it naturally, thinks in its terms, and sometimes lives by its values. Given those gaps, many parents give up. This leaves the child alone facing the multiple dangers of the virtual world. In the face of that threat, parents have no choice but to develop initiatives to restore their parenthood and develop a stance of vigilant care.

The main risks can be divided into two areas: (1) content and interactions, such as exposure to harmful sites, exploitation by predators, or victimization on the social networks; and (2) withdrawal from the real world and getting swallowed up into the virtual world.

Supervising Internet Use

Given the difficulties and the depth of their helplessness, many parents would be surprised to learn that it might take only a relatively short time to develop a method of supervision that will significantly reduce their sense of alienation and the risks to which their children are exposed. Our studies have found that after brief training parents were able to stop feeling that everything their children were experiencing in the virtual world was alien, acquired a sense that they were on top of the situation, and were able to act to reduce harmful activities.

Like the other areas we discussed so far, the distinction between control and vigilant care proves to be critical. It is clear parents cannot achieve control, both because their children are more proficient than they on this subject and because the virtual world is accessible from everywhere. The attempt to control the flood of opportunities facing the child is like trying to block the sea. However, parents can still exercise vigilant care, serve as lighthouses for their children, indicate danger areas, and drop anchors that curb dangerous drifting. Parental vigilance induces self-vigilance by children, which will help them care for themselves in the present and the future. To do this, parents must develop basic familiarity with the dangers of the internet.

The Dangers of the Internet: A Quick Guide for Parents

The main areas where children are exposed to online risks are as follows:

- Temptation to engage in forbidden actions such as sexual exploitation, seduction into destructive activities (such as drugs, gambling, anorexia), and attempts at recruitment into harmful groups,
- Temptation to shop and make financial commitments—children can enter commitments through their smartphone accounts without even requiring credit card details. This can happen through theft of personal information such as credit card details or passwords.
- Online violence such as attempts to shame and hurt people on social networks or invitations to group boycotts.
- Harmful self-exposure that will lead to harm in the present or future.
- Viruses or Trojan horses inserted into the computer in order to damage it, influence its contents, or steal information.
- Exposure to age-inappropriate contents, such as pornography.
- Bullying.

Step One in Supervising of Internet Use: Discussion

The first step in parents' taking a vigilant stance in the virtual realm is for them to initiate a discussion with the child. We strongly recommend a formal and structured discussion, among other reasons because the importance and risks in this area exceed anything that can be addressed by an incidental conversation. The formal discussion we propose can last two hours, which can be divided into two sessions. We recommend that at the end of the discussion the parent and child sign a contract that defines mutual commitments. The signing of the contract is appropriate for the area of computer and smartphone use because when you provide opportunities that contain a risk, it is important to condition the provisioning of those opportunities on a commitment designed to prevent potential harm. The signing of the contract gives the parent explicit justification to increase supervision if and when the child does not meet contractual terms. The contract also increases the chances that the child will think of his or her parents when facing the temptations, the contract describes. The discussion we propose is divided into two parts:

Discussion Part One

Part One starts with a guided tour of the child's computer activity. The parent announces, "I want to get to know the ways you use your computer and smartphone and to reach an understanding with you about basic safety rules." If parents deliver this announcement in a clear and unequivocal way, the chances of cooperation will be high. The clearer it is to parents that having this discussion is a crucial duty, the more they will project the requisite determination when they approach the child. From our experience, it is rare for a child to refuse to have such a conversation with a parent. When that does happen, the parent can rest assured that the child is making harmful use of the virtual world, which requires the parent to move to a more intensive level of vigilant care.

The first part of the discussion is devoted to the child showing the parents various activities on their computer and smartphone, such as games, Facebook, chats, and favorite sites. The parents will let the child lead them on a kind of guided tour (like showing a tourist a foreign country). The parents show interest rather than attempting an interrogation. They ask the child to show them his or her favorite games. If there are complicated online games, the parents will ask for explanations and demonstrations. Genuine interest in the games the child plays can contribute to creating a good atmosphere and getting to know the child's online activity. The parents should not be satisfied by a general description such as "I play all kinds of role-playing games." If the conversation were about sports, no parent would be satisfied with an answer like "I play some game with a ball." Likewise, parents should ask for a much more detailed picture of the games which occupy their child's computer time. The child will be surprised and usually react positively when finding that the parents' questions reflect genuine interest.

Parents who are not their child's Facebook friend can ask the child to show them his or her Facebook page. If the child hesitates, the parents can suggest the child make changes on the Facebook page so that he or she can show it to the parents without fear. This reinforces to the child that the parents are indeed interested in the child's activities and reduces a sense of being interrogated.

The purpose of the talk is not to obtain information about problematic activities but to increase the parents' positive presence in their child's life, particularly their child's computer life. Parents also can ask the child to show them favorite sites. They can say reassuringly, "Show me only the sites that you feel comfortable showing me." They can also ask the child about the use of smartphone applications and inquire about recent innovations. In some cases, parents can ask the child to help them install for themselves and teach them how to use an application that seems relevant to them.

Discussion Part Two

Part two begins with a talk about risks and restrictions. In this part of the discussion, the parent moves to questions about the risks we enumerated above. We suggest using a list of questions prepared in advance. A parent who comes to the meeting equipped with such a list indicates the importance of the conversation. Otherwise, a flowing and spontaneous talk may actually undermine the seriousness of the discussion. Following is a recommended list of questions that address the different risks:

- Contacts:
  - "Has a stranger ever tried to contact you?"
  - "Has anyone ever tried to interest you in forbidden activities?"

If the child says no or doesn't understand the question, the parents should ask by way of explanation:

- "Have there been attempts to interest you in gambling, drugs, or sexual activities?"
- "How do you exercise caution against that?"
- "Has anyone ever written to you in a way that made you feel uncomfortable?"
- "What will you do if that happens?"

Following the questions, parents should clarify their position simply and quietly, without threatening or preaching: "You can understand why I'm asking these questions. Many children have been tempted into harmful meetings or activities. I want you know that if anything like that happens, I will support you and help you protect yourself or get out of trouble. If anything like that happens, tell me, and I promise I will not be angry but support you."

- Purchases:
  - "Have you bought anything online or with your smartphone?"
  - "Have you downloaded for-pay applications?"
  - "Have you ever given out our credit card details?"

After briefly dwelling on these questions, parents should add, "It is very important to be careful because a commitment through your smartphone or online can lead to a situation it is very hard to get out of."

The parents should then summarize their position by saying, "We want to agree with you that if you get our consent to buy something with our credit card, it applies exclusively only to that purchase. We, of course, check the charges on our credit card, but you need to know how to avoid getting into such inextricable situations."

- Identity theft:
  - "Has anyone tried to get you to give them your username and password?"
  - "Often, outside parties try to get your information, supposedly in order to improve the services they give you, but it is a false pretense: their real goal is to obtain your username and password. Has anyone asked you for this information, saying that they want to improve your service?"

After briefly raising these issues, the parents add, "Please do not ever give your username and password unless you are 100% sure of who you're giving them to. Don't respond to any request for information about you by email or text. It's almost always for pernicious purposes."

- Bullying:
  - "Has anyone insulted you or slandered you on Facebook or another social network?"
  - "Have such things happened to your friends?"
  - "Your classmates?"
  - "Has there ever been an attempt to boycott someone you know on Facebook?"
  - "How would you respond if such a thing happened?"

After quickly going over these questions, the parent should explain, "I need you to know how to protect yourself and how not to get caught up in online bullying or boycotts. If such a thing happens, you must tell me. I promise to help! And if you ever do get into trouble, I will do everything I can to help you without shaming you."

- Exposure:
  - "Many times, children expose things about themselves on Facebook or blogs that they are sorry about later. Do you think any of your friends have exposed anything they might be sorry about in the future?"
  - "Do you think anyone exposed things that can hurt them in the future, like when they look for a job?"
  - "If friends exposed something you thought was problematic, would you be willing to warn them if you thought it was inappropriate?"

After briefly going over these questions, the parents should add, "It is important for you to know that things that you reveal about yourself can hurt you in the future. There are companies that specialize in collecting such information, and one day you may discover that outside parties know things about you that you wouldn't want them to know. We want to make sure you know how to be careful and not get tempted by the urge to expose things about yourself in order to get a sympathetic response or to impress others. Such things can cost you dearly."

- Viruses:
  - "How do you protect yourself against viruses?"
  - "Has your computer ever been infected by a virus? What did you do?"

After briefly going over this, the parents add, "Do not open any message if you are not completely sure who sent it. Sometimes, even a message from someone you know can be harmful. If there is anything weird about the subject, something that doesn't seem suitable to the person who supposedly sent it, don't open it."

- Illicit sites:
  - "Have you come across pornography?"
  - If the child denies ever having seen any pornographic materials: "If you haven't run into it yet, you will for sure, if not on your computer than on your friends' computers. How do you think you will respond if you're invited to look at such sites?"
  - "Have you run into sites that offer gambling?"
  - "How would you respond to that?"
  - "Have you come across sites that glorify drugs or crazy diets?"
  - "How would you respond to that?"

After briefly going over these questions, the parents should add, "There are tons of sites that overwhelm you with pornography. I know you're going to run into it, it's inevitable these days. I want you to know that pornography is not like healthy sex. It's completely fake. These people are not enjoying themselves but doing it only for money or for drugs. You should know that pornography is one big lie! Also, you must not be tempted by sites that try to seduce you into gambling, drugs, crazy diets, and other dangerous things. If such things are offered to you, it is very important for us to know. Trust us that we will do everything we can to help you."

Some parents will be reluctant to ask these questions so directly and systematically. They might prefer a more spontaneous and freestyle conversation instead of a formal discussion in which they go from item to item like a lawyer reviewing a legal document. As we said when we described the announcement process, the formality is deliberate and is a key element of the event, serving as a rite of passage between the previous era of permissiveness and a new era in which the parents wish to be involved. The very fact that the parents prepare themselves for the talk and come with a list of subjects, questions, and clarifications about their position changes their degree of presence. Now, the chance that the child will think of them if and when one of those scenarios occurs is higher. That presence in the child's mind is the ultimate object of parental vigilant care.

Discussion Part Three

The last part of the discussion is devoted to attempting to reach a written agreement on the rules of use of the computer and smartphone. Parents might say, "We've never spoken clearly about ways to make sure you're not hurt by your use of the virtual world, but we've reached the conclusion it's necessary. We provide you with your computer, smartphone, and Internet service, and we must make sure you do not use them harmfully. So, we want to ask you to sign an agreement with us that will protect all of us. I got this proposal from experts on safe computer and internet use. Please read it and tell me if you want to add anything."

Parent-Child Agreement on Safe Computer Use

The parents' commitment:

We, the parents, undertake to maintain an open and respectful dialogue with you about the limits of your computer and smartphone use, out of trust and recognition of the importance of these tools for all of our lives. We will oversee your online activities out of our duty as parents to protect you. All of our activity on this matter will be undertaken openly.

The child' commitment:_

1. I will provide no information about myself and my family such as: name, address, phone number, etc., without my parents' approval.

2. I will tell my parents immediately if I am approached in any way that makes me feel threatened or uncomfortable.

3. I will not meet/make an appointment with a strange person I met online without checking with my parents. Only if my parents agree will I make such an appointment and only in a public place.

4. I will not send my picture to a strange person or body without my parents' approval.

5. I will not react or respond to any message that makes me feel uncomfortable.

6. I will not surf on any website I promise not to. I will not enter websites with pornography, gambling, or sites that recommend drugs or other harmful activities.

7. I will not participate in any bullying or boycotting activity. If I become witness to such events, I'll think if there is anything that can be done in order to stop it. I'll think whom I could report it to, so as to rescue the victim from danger

8. I will not use my computer or smartphone in a way that detracts from my sleep time, school attendance, or functioning as a student. I will not use my computer at the expense of family activities such as meals, family visits or family outings.

Signed:

____________________ ____________________

____________________ ____________________

Signing the contract signals commitment but in itself is not a guarantee that the child will honor all of its terms. If the child does not, the parents are far from helpless. The contract adds legitimacy to measures the parents take if the contract is not fulfilled. If, on the other hand, the child refuses to sign the contract, that is in itself a warning that indicates problematic use and requires parental intervention.

If parents feel that the process we suggested seems cumbersome and embarrassing to them and that they prefer to keep things as they are, they must ask themselves whether they are not neglecting their parental obligations in a critical area of their and their children's lives. The virtual world has become the main place where many children evade parental oversight. Parents' return to the position of vigilant care signals a far-reaching change that fundamentally resets both the parents' position and the child's safety level.

Neglect of Real-World Activities in Favor of Virtual-World Absorption

The second danger that faces children doesn't have to do with the contents or contacts created in the virtual world but with their abandoning their activities in the real world in favor of the computer screen or the telephone. This has many manifestations: increasing disengagement from their familial and social environment, a drop in school performance, increased seclusion, detraction from sleep, deterioration in physical condition, and at times, a complete abandonment of all interaction in the real world in favor of exclusive absorption in the virtual world.

Many parents ask how much and how to restrict computer and smartphone use. Experience shows that limiting the number of hours a day the child is allowed to use the computer or phone is ineffective. Such restrictions put the parents in the role of police who count the hours and then enter into endless arguments about it with their child. The atmosphere of constant bargaining harms the relationship and exhausts the parents. On the other hand, parents are much more successful at establishing a number of clear and simple rules such as no smartphones during meals, no smartphones before leaving for school, and no tech after 10 PM. The advantage of these rules is that they are much clearer and do not tend to be eroded by the endless bargaining that characterizes putting limits on the permitted number of hours of use of technology.

Parents should not think they can maintain limits without systematic preparation. The attempt to impose limits on use of technology through verbal demands and threats of punishment is doomed to failure. That is because the technological world has such an overwhelming and sweeping presence in the child's life that the parents' protestations can fail to leave a mark. Not so when the parents approach the task with the necessary patience and gravity. To do so, they should coordinate their positions between them, define the limits, announce them unequivocally (advisedly by a formal announcement), build backing and legitimacy through supporters, and prepare for decisive action if and when the limits are violated.

Benny and Gloria attended a lecture on problematic computer and telephone use. Following the lecture, they consulted the speaker on how to change their children's habit of getting absorbed in their smartphones during meals, which had become an unpleasant routine in their family. In their talk with the speaker, both parents agreed to make it a high priority to liberate their family meals from smartphones. They prepared a written announcement, gathered their three children, ages 15, 14 and 10 around the table, and told them, "Recently, our meals have stopped being family occasions. Instead, they have become a collection of separate people absorbed in their smartphone. We have decided together we are going to do whatever we can to change this situation that is very damaging to our family spirit. Mom and I are not going to turn our phones on anymore or answer phone calls during meals. We have decided this rule will apply to you as well. There will be no more smartphones at the table. We are going to demand that you turn your phones off so that there will be no rings during meals. We are going to enforce this rule absolutely. We have shared this decision with your grandparents, your two aunts, and their children so that when we have a meal at our house everyone will have to turn off their phones before the meal."

The three children received written copies of the announcement. The announcement was delivered an hour before dinner. Before the meal, the parents turned off their phones in their children's presence and asked them to do the same. Nobody objected.

The parents asked the grandparents to maintain the same rule when they hosted Friday-night dinners. The fact that the ceremony of turning off the phones took place at the grandparents' house as well significantly reinforced the parents' rule.

Gloria's younger sister was very impressed by the decision and the way it was carried out, and she adopted the same rule for her family. Benny's sister did not feel the need for a similar restriction in her house, but she agreed to maintain the rule every time she and her children came for dinner at Benny and Gloria's.

When the warning signals indicate to parents that their child is using the computer illegitimately, they must move to the ultimate level of vigilant care, namely unilateral measures to protect the child. Here are some questions parents can ask themselves to assess whether there are warning signs that justify determined intervention:

- Does my child lock the door when he or she is on the computer?
- Does my child sit in front of a screen until late at night?
- Does my child make unauthorized charges on our credit card?
- Does my child neglect school in favor of Internet activities?
- Does my child avoid meals and other family activities in favor of the computer?
- Has my child curtailed social activities outside of home in favor of the computer?
- Does my child scream at us when we interrupt him or her on the computer?
- Does my child refuse to answer questions about his or her computer use?

These are all warning signs that justify you in tightening your vigilant care. Do not do these things impulsively and do not expect threats or punishments to solve the problem. The best way to launch the process is by a formal announcement. Following is a possible format for such an announcement:

We know how important the computer is in your life, but we've recently noticed that your use detracts from good performance in things like school and sleep. So, we are going to do whatever we can to reduce that harm and make sure your computer use is constructive and not destructive.

If the child refuses to read the announcement or protests vocally, the parent should say quietly, "I didn't expect you to agree. I gave you this copy to be fair and not do anything behind your back. This announcement expresses my supreme duty as a parent and the fact that I am not going to give up on you." After this statement, the parent should end the discussion to prevent the development of a pointless argument. Below are some practical steps parents can take to put an end to destructive computer use.

Ending Destructive Computer Habits

Restricting screen time

Parents must set a time after which there will be no computer use. If the child does not accept the cutoff time, parents must shut the computer down themselves. The parent should not turn the computer off while the child is sitting in front of it. This often leads to serious and even violent escalation of conflict.

There are several ways to move forward without falling into that trap. For instance, tell the child that if the computer is not turned off immediately, it will be disabled. In this case, the parents should disable the computer when the child isn't present, for instance by removing a functional component (modem or mouse).

Another way is to tell the child: "You have five minutes to save your contents and turn the computer off. Afterward, we are going to make sure it is shut down." If the child doesn't turn it off, do not approach and press the button, but cut the electricity for a few seconds.

In the case of a smartphone, parents should exercise patience in preventing illegitimate use, such as by cutting off the Wi-Fi. This can be done most effectively when backed by a supporter. A supporter can tell the child in advance that the parents are going to turn off the electricity.

If the parents anticipate that the child will react violently, they should shut down the computer the next day and leave it that way until the child commits to following the rules strictly. In such cases involving supporters is particularly important. Supporters help in three ways:

- preventing escalation;
- backing parents' positions; and
- making the child's commitment in front of them more binding than a commitment made only in front of the parents.

Cutting off Access

Sometimes, it is recommended to cut off the Internet for a while. This is not easy and demands parental commitment and advance preparation. In many cases the child also uses the Internet for positive and even necessary activities (such as downloading homework from the school website). In these cases, the parents should plan for alternative solutions for the duration of the internet being shut down. One possibility of which many parents are not aware is ordering Internet service that is limited to certain hours of the day. Remember that if the child is used to spending days and nights in front of the computer, they will react severely to cutting off the internet. It will be hard for the child to find alternative activities and sometimes they will feel as if their entire contact with their social life has been cut off. Despite the resistance, our experience with hundreds of families shows that any parent can do these things if they prepare in advance and recruit supporters. We would like to emphasize that the terrible scenarios parents fear do not materialize. Yes, cutting off the Internet and shutting down the computer will be met with fierce resistance by some children, but planned and determined action by parents elevates their authority and lowers the risk of the child engaging in difficult activities.

Confiscating the Smartphone

This is a measure that evokes intense fears in many parents. Many perceive the smartphone as almost the natural extension of the child and its confiscation as the violation of a sacred taboo. Parents are also afraid of what will happen if they are unable to contact their child when they are away from home. Therefore, it is necessary to prepare thoroughly for confiscating the smartphone and not do it impulsively.

The parents' right to confiscate the smartphone is related to their assessment that the child is using it in a way that causes harm. When parents reach this conclusion and when other measures such as limiting hours of use and increasing supervision do not help, confiscating the smartphone is justified. In most of the cases in which we accompanied parents through this process, the confiscation was temporary, usually for a few days, or, in a handful of cases, for a few weeks or months.

In a few cases, teenagers bought new smartphones and paid for their expenses with their own money. In those cases, the parents told the children they would not let them use the smartphone in their home because it is their duty not to allow destructive activities. Just as they would not let their child use dangerous drugs at home, so, too, parents must resist any other risky activity in their home, such as the abuse of a smartphone.

Confiscation of the smartphone should not be carried out by a physical struggle in an attempt to overcome the child's resistance. Such an attempt could lead to an outburst of violence.

One possibility is to demand the smartphone be turned over in the presence of supporters. Some parents informed their child that if they used the smartphone at home, they would confiscate it. Later, the parents took it away while the child was sleeping. Even in these cases, the involvement of supporters plays a significant role because a supporter can explain to the child that the parents' action was justified and an agreement to give it back can be reached if the child is ready to commit to required restrictions. Sometimes, parents are surprised to what extent their child is willing to accept the terms they refused to even hear about from them, if the proposal is raised in a dignified way by a third party. As for parents' fear that they will not be able to call their child when they are away from home, they must prepare for this just like for a telephone tree. In other words, they collect in advance the phone numbers of friends and other people who are in touch with their child. Such preparation will enable the parents to look for their child and demonstrate presence much more effectively than communicating through the smartphone.

Simon and René watched helplessly as their daughter Rhea, 16, dropped out of school, spent days and nights on Facebook and her smartphone, and at the same time developed an attitude of con-

tempt and alienation toward them. When their therapist suggested that they resist the process of her disengagement and take determined action to reduce Rhea's activity in the virtual world, Simon cried, "That is an extreme approach. It's as if you asked me to cut off my daughter's arm! How do I know it won't lead to depression or her doing something drastic?"

Later in the conversation it became clear that Rhea had never threatened to harm herself and was not at all depressed. The therapist explained that even had there been such threats, the way to cope with them would not be to maintain the sanctity of Rhea's virtual world at the expense of her normal life. The therapist focused on the phrase "cut off my daughter's arm," which expressed an exaggerated fear and the father's sense of illegitimacy of any action related to the smartphone.

After a process in which the parents prepared for different scenarios of strong resistance by their daughter, they made an announcement, intensified their supervision, and when none of this led to progress, cut off the computer, and confiscated the smartphone. To their surprise, all of Rhea's resistance was limited to the stages before the disconnection, in an attempt to prevent it. Once she saw that her parents really did carry through these actions, she immediately entered into negotiations. The negotiations went on for more than two weeks, and for the whole time the computer stayed off and Rhea remained without a smartphone.

The reason discussions went on so long was that the parents, with the help of supporters, demanded clear indications that Rhea was performing well as a student. After the computer and smartphone were restored, there was a difficult period of adjustment, but Rhea's functional impairment and absorption in the virtual world were vastly reduced. When at the end of the process the therapist went back to the metaphor of cutting off her arm, which Simon had used at the beginning of the process, the father said, "I can't believe I thought that. As if the smartphone were as sacred as my daughter's life!"

***

Abed and Nida were the parents of Mark, 14, who until the last year had been an excellent student, active in the Scouts, and surrounded by friends. Nothing warned his parents of the profound change in his life when he started playing one of the compelling online games that were popular at the time. Within a few months Mark had disengaged from almost all social activity. He left the Scouts, and his grades deteriorated at school, He started showing up late and leaving early on false pretenses in order to sit in the park for an hour or two and play his game on his smartphone before going home and secluding himself with his computer until the wee hours of the morning. His relationship with his parents, which had previously been good, completely deteriorated, being reduced to endless arguments about the game.

The parents prepared an announcement, which was delivered to Mark in his room in the presence not only of his parents but also two grandparents, an uncle, an aunt, and an older cousin, Roy, whom Mark admired. In the announcement, the parents said they would do everything they could to fight against the game's taking over Mark's life. The supporters reinforced the parents' message.

After the meeting, Roy invited Mark to go to a café with him because he wanted to help him find a solution that was acceptable to him. Mark went with him willingly. After a 2-hour discussion they wrote a joint proposal. Mark promised in writing not to play the game before finishing all of his school work for that day. He agreed not to turn on the computer until after dinner and in the presence of a parent or one of the supporters, whose job was to write down the beginning time of the game and warn Mark 15 minutes before three hours were up. He committed to turning off the computer when he got the message. Mark also committed not to play the game on his smartphone and agreed that if he violated that commitment, he would lose the right to have a smartphone as well as the right to have a computer in his room.

Roy planned a program with Mark to catch up on missed schoolwork. Within two months, Mark had come back to himself, and all the life areas he had neglected had returned to normal. The big surprise was that he decided himself that the game had ruined his life. Within a short time, the agreement on the terms of computer use became superfluous because Mark stopped playing the game on his own.

Conclusion

The computer and smartphone are probably the main causes of erosion of parental presence in our age. They reduce dialogue, prevent contact, and bring in any number of unmitigated influences on the child's life. Parents' return to enactment of vigilant care enables them to deal with the challenge on different levels. When there are no signs of problematic use, parents should show interest in the child's activity in the virtual world, ask for a "guided tour," and show them they are happy to learn from the child about the child's computer use and skill. Parents should also have a structured meeting with the child about the dangers of the Internet. It is advisable to culminate this process with the signing of a contract. This request is not foreign to children because often, when they download an application, they are asked to check a box confirming they accept its terms. Effective vigilant care in the virtual world presumes a willingness to intervene resolutely, if necessary. A number of factors give parents the requisite strength to do so: the recognition of signs of risk (deterioration in the child's scholastic, social and familial performance), a systematic plan to limit Internet service, and the mobilization of support for measures to be implemented. When parents prepare, they can prevent illegitimate use even in cases when the problem has already reached extremely serious dimensions. Parents who learn how to serve as anchors against the drift of the child into a virtual world will be able to act decidedly also in other areas of risk.

Review and Application

- Parents must manifest their presence in the virtual world to which their child is exposed.
- Do not expect commands, threats, or punishments to achieve results. It is necessary to act with a deep breath and determination.

- A request for a "guided tour" of the child's virtual world will usually be accepted.
- Prepare for a planned and structured discussion, in which you ask how your child protects himself or herself against the dangers of the virtual world.
- It is advisable to sign a contract of protected use.
- The planned discussion and signing of the contract increase your mental presence in the virtual world.
- When signs of risk appear, prepare to move to a more intensive vigilant care.
- Declare limits unequivocally.
- Prepare to reduce Internet service.
- Recruit support for your position.
- Do not turn off the computer while the child is sitting in front of it.
- Do not wrest the cellphone out of a child's hands.
- Remember! The computer, cellphone, and Internet are services you supply, but they should be used in legitimate ways. If they become destructive, it is your duty to stop supplying them.

Conclusion

The Threat and the Vision

We began this book with the statement that the role of parenthood has become much less clear in the present generation. We described how parents' lack of clarity intersects with changes in the family, society, and technology, eroding their ability to function and withstand the pressures. Nothing is a better immunizer against confusion, perplexity, and drifting than a rallying vision translated into a concrete plan. It takes some daring to formulate such a vision today, but if we don't develop such a vision, we may be destined to drift this way and that, without a compass or a map. Therefore, I presume to present my vision even if it elicits a smirk from some of my readers.

- Where there was parental impulsiveness, there will be self-control. We have shown in our studies that even parents who were highly impulsive and haphazard have the capacity to collect themselves, control their reactions, and respond with restraint to challenging situations and severe provocations. The rise in self-control has proven to be a key factor in improving the child's behavior and the home atmosphere.

- Where there was parental loneliness and isolation, there will be a support network for the parent and child. The understanding that seclusion within the closed and secret bubble of a nuclear family weakens parents and increases the risks facing the child drives many parents to be willing to be helped by others. In our work with parents, we showed how to overcome typical reservations such as the privacy reflex, feelings of shame, the false belief that asking for help indicates weakness, and the misconception that no significant support can be found. We showed that parents who are willing to reach out overcome their paralysis and helplessness. By doing so, they create a new environment which, instead of perpetuating the child's problems, opens channels to real improvement. This provides the parents with reinforcement and legitimacy.

- Where there was parental erosion and marginality, there will be presence and vigilant care. We described the change that occurred in families where the parents acted to reclaim their role in leading their children as "the return of the parent." We showed that even when children protest, they also have inner voices that approve of the parents' actions. Increasing presence and improving vigilant care have been demonstrated to reduce all kinds of risks at all ages.

- Where chaos reigned, a loving parental limit will be set. We showed how the loving limit is much more than a sanction. The parents do not simply set a limit for their child, but become themselves the limit. We described various ways parents can make the change so that interactions that were once merely disciplinary become existential experiences of a loving limit, which significantly changes the living conditions of all the members of the household.

- Where there was fickleness, there will be persistence and continuity. The experience of parental hassle, expressed by a frenetic movement among prohibitions, shouting, scolding, threatening and frustration, can gradually be crystallized into that of a coherent, consistent, and persistent parenting. Instead of a scattering of "no's" that dissipate and burst like bubbles, parents learn how to hold to their red lines. Time itself turns into a basis of stable parenting. The ability to delay reaction or to come back to a subject later, remember and persist, provide consistency and order where the child's and parents' inner experience was chaotic and capricious.

- Where there was distance and disengagement there will be connection and belonging. The weakening of the family is clearly seen by the decline in feelings of belonging. Children and adolescents become increasingly absorbed into their computers and smartphones, marginal groups, and hidden activities. Parents who show presence and are able to connect with a support network can become a source of attraction for the child's need of belonging. The renewal of family affiliation is one of the most salient features of our approach and vision.

Those principles are the heart of my vision. But one always wishes to distill one's vision into a unifying image. Although each chapter in this book describes a new angle, I hope at the end the reader will come out not only with a collection of tips but also with a unifying image of how to maintain their parenthood against the countless demands and challenges of this complex age. If a picture can be worth a thousand words, then the following image depicts my whole attempt:

Where there was drifting, there will be anchoring. Parental anchoring is expressed by resolute presence, self-control, connection with supporters, and the determined caring of the warm loving. The symbol of parental authority is no longer the raised fist, the angry face, the threatening shout, or the severe punishment but the present, stable, connected, and connecting anchor.

Select MSI Books

Childhood Memoirs

Good Blood (Schaffer)

It Only Hurts When I Can't Run (Parker)

Of God, Rattlesnakes, and Okra (Easterling)

One Family: Indivisible (Greenebaum)

Tucker and Me (Harvey)

Health & Fitness

100 Tips and Tools for Managing Chronic Illness (Charnas)

108 Yoga and Self-Care Practices for Busy Mommas (Gentile)

Girl, You Got This! (Renz)

Living Well with Chronic Illness (Charnas)

Survival of the Caregiver (Snyder)

The Optimistic Food Addict (Fisanick)

Parenting & Teaching

365 Teacher Secrets for Parents: Fun Ways to Help Your Child in Elementary School (McKinley & Trombly)

Courageous Parents (Omer)

How to Be a Good Mommy When You're Sick (Graves)

Lessons of Labor (Aziz)

Life after Losing a Child (Young & Romer)

Noah's New Puppy (Rice, with Henderson)

Soccer Is Fun without Parents (Jonas)

The Invisible Foreign Language Classroom (Dabbs & Leaver)

Understanding the Challenge of "No" for Children with Autism (McNeil)

Psychology & Philosophy

Anger Anonymous: The Big Book on Anger Addiction (Ortman)

Anxiety Anonymous: The Big Book on Anxiety Addiction (Ortman)

Awesome Couple Communication (Pickett)

Depression Anonymous: The Big Book on Depression Addiction (Ortman)

El Poder de lo Transpersonal (Ustman)

From Deep Within (Lewis)

How to Live from Your Heart (Hucknall)

Road Map to Power (Husain & Husain)

The Marriage Whisperer: How to Improve Your Relationship Overnight (Pickett)

The Power of Grief (Potter)

The Rose and the Sword: How to Balance Your Feminine and Masculine Energies (Bach & Hucknall)

The Seven Wisdoms of Life (Tubali)

Understanding the Analyst: Socionics in Everyday Life (Quinelle)

Understanding the Critic: Socionics in Everyday Life (Quinelle)

Understanding the Entrepreneur: Socionics in Everyday Life (Quinelle)

Understanding the People around You: An Introduction to Socionics (Filatova)

Understanding the Romantic (Quinelle)

Understanding the Seeker: Socionics in Everyday Life (Quinelle)

CPSIA information can be obtained
at www.ICGtesting.com
Printed in the USA
BVHW041802160621
609642BV00002B/303